Many a Summer

Many a Summer

The story of George (1893-1984)

Hardiman Scott

an
IMAGES
publication

Many a Summer

First published in Great Britain 1991.
Reprinted October 1992

Copyright © Hardiman Scott 1991

ISBN 0 948134 32 1

RICHARD CASTELL PUBLISHING LIMITED
24 Queens Road Lipson Plymouth PL4 7PL

Designed & Typeset by Castell Design & Print of Plymouth

*The front cover illustration is taken from a painting entitled
'Following the plough' by Lucy Kemp-Welch R.I.,R.O.I.,R.B. (1869-1958)*

Printed by W.B.C. Print Limited
Waterton Industrial Estate Bridgend Mid-Glamorgan CF31 3YN

Hardiman Scott

During the sixties and seventies, Hardiman Scott was a familiar face on television, and just as well-known on radio, when he made hundreds of broadcasts as the BBC's first political correspondent, and then their first political editor. He took a leading role in negotiating the radio broadcasting of Parliament when MPs were still refusing to let in the television cameras. The last five years of his long career with the BBC were spent as Chief Assistant to the Director-General. He was also one of the four-man BBC team that went to Zimbabwe to advise on the reorganization of broadcasting after that country's independence. For eight years he was also a founder-member of the Broadcasting Complaints Commission. Since his retirement from the BBC, he has added to his reputation as both poet and novelist. He was awarded the OBE in 1989. An East Anglian by birth and upbringing, Hardiman Scott lives in Suffolk.

For Sue
and to the memory of
George Everett

The woods decay, the woods decay and fall,
The vapours weep their burthen to the ground,
Man comes and tills the field and lies beneath,
And after many a summer dies the swan.

- Tennyson *(Tithonus)*

Contents

Foreword

George Everett was born in the last decade of the nineteenth century, and he has lived in the same area of Suffolk ever since. Most of his working life he was a farm labourer. The only time he has been away from Suffolk was during his service in the first world war.

Like many of his comrades he showed great courage. He is a kindly and gentle man with a native shrewdness and quiet dignity, but he has no special claims to distinction. That, however, is what is important.

His conversation is about another age - its life, its work, its hardships and its satisfactions, its values and its assumptions. There are other men like George all over Britain, but naturally they are becoming fewer and fewer. With their passing we lose the living links with a different world. In one of the richest farming areas of the country - sometimes known as the grain and sugar bowl of Britain - he is the link between the old ways of the country and the new, the old farming and the technology of today.

So this book is an attempt to preserve something of that link through the character of a farm labourer in the early years of this century. In the process, it is, for most part, the story of George's life. Mostly, I have told it in his words, recorded in many hours of conversation.

Except rarely (for example, the occasional feller for fellow) I have not written his words phonetically (not even owd for old) in an attempt to capture the rich sound of his Suffolk voice. I have, however, tried to preserve something of the cadence of his speech by using his own phrases, with their occasional dialect word, and his characteristic Suffolk mannerisms. There are sometimes passages of description or explanation, but where, in the narrative of his life, the words are not in quotes, what I have written is based entirely on what George has told me.

I have tried to keep footnotes to a minimum, and wherever possible have put brief explanations in brackets in the text. References to Moor, Forby and Claxton are to 'Suffolk Words and Phrases' by Edward Moor (1823), the 'Vocabulary of East Anglia' by Robert Forby (1830) and 'The Suffolk Dialect of the Twentieth Century' by A.O.D.Claxton (1968). All other necessary references are detailed in the text or footnotes.

1
Childhood

The night George was born his father, returning home across the fields, fell over a snow-covered horse in the farmyard. Neither took any harm, either from the fall or the snow. When he was a schoolboy George often got a lift home on the back of that same 'quiet old horse'.

David Henry Everett - 'Dick' as all his fellow farmworkers called him - was no more than medium height and slight of build, but he gave an impression of strength. His face, with its sideburns, well-set jaw and large nose, contributed to the rugged appearance. On this occasion he had walked downhill from his home to the village of Boxford. It lies about two hundred feet below, in the valley of the river Box, a snug collection of mainly Tudor houses grouped about the early fifteenth-century church. Together they are the remaining evidence of the medieval prosperity of this wool 'town' of West Suffolk. It got its name - probably in the fifth or sixth century - from the river crossing where the box trees grew. There are still box trees growing on the bank of the river that flows through the middle of the village.

What Dick Everett was doing there on the last night of 1892 is not known for certain. It might be reasonable to assume that, after a hard week's work, he had gone to join some of his mates for a well-deserved pint at the Fleece or The White Hart, but since The Brewer's Arms was hard by the Brewery Cottages in which he lived at Bower House Tye, it seems unlikely that he would choose such a hard, cold night for a walk of almost two miles by road into the village. It is more likely that he had made the journey to summon the doctor. Whatever the reason, there was at least a foot of snow on the ground when Dick Everett chose the shorter route uphill across the fields back to his home.

Behind the cottages lay Bower House Farm, where he was employed. He stumbled across the farmyard in the driving snow. Earlier in the day fodder had been spread across the yard. Dick strode through what he imagined to be a heap of it, only to fall headlong in the snow over the resting body of the horse.

It was almost midnight when he got home. His wife, Betsy Jane, who was nearly thirty-five, was in labour with her fifth child. The doctor had already come up from Boxford by horse and sleigh.

About five minutes into the new year of 1893 George Albert Everett was born. Not only Suffolk but most of Europe was covered with snow. Within two days the Thames was frozen over above the tideway.

It was a hard beginning to what was to become a hard but enjoyable life. The cottage where he was born already housed, in addition to his parents, his eldest brother, William, who was nine-and-a-half; Jack, who was eight; Arthur, aged six; and Ruth, who was five years old. Three more - Morris, Mary and Charles - were to follow George.

All ten lived in the brick cottage of two rooms up and two down. There was no bathroom, and the water supply came from a pump outside at the end of the house. Its proximity was a convenience for the Everetts, because it served three cottages. There was, however, never a shortage of water. Other pumps were about thirty and fifty yards away, and there was a fourth by The Brewer's Arms, evidently all drawing water from the same spring. The children were washed in a large tin bath. Water was carried from the pump to the boiler or cauldron, heated up, and then carried again to the bath.

His mother also used the boiler for the weekly wash. It held several gallons of water, and was heated over an open fireplace. It stood over two rods of iron resting on bricks, with the fire beneath. All the washing, from small items of clothing to sheets, was done by hand with common soap.

George says, 'She used to rub everything by hand. That was jolly hard work for a woman, especially with a large family. As a child, I would watch my mother a-working, and I thought a lot about her, poor old girl, and the way she slaved for us to keep things clean. She was only a tiny woman too. And with our family there'd perhaps be six or seven bed-sheets at a time. She would ring out most things by hand. But she did have a mangle, and sometimes she'd put the sheets and towels through that. But I don't say that was all done in one day. She might do all the big stuff she could in one go, and then do the others another day. She dried them all outside on the line. That was about twenty yards long.'

After a big wash the boilers would be wiped out and cleaned, and would be fit for the occasional wine making.

The cottages had brick floors. They were left bare in the kitchen, and were regularly scrubbed by George's mother. In their tiny living-room the bricks formed a border round the rug floor coverings. The furniture was sparse but practical - country-made chairs and table, and horsehair sofa. The chairs, like the table, are still in use. Sturdy, well-shaped, they have the golden colour of old maple. They were made for Dick Everett when he got married by a carpenter in the neighbouring village of Groton. They cost thirteen shillings and sixpence each (65 1/2p).

'These old chairs have took some hammering with all us children, but they'll last several generations yet, that they will. Furniture was better then than it is today. Youngsters, nowadays, they have a front room, and they don't go and sit in it. They've just got the stuff in there, and they look at it. They daren't use it.'

The cottages were lit by oil lamps. Oil was cheap and was obtained from a neighbour, Mrs Barnes.

'She lived just below us, and you could go there and get oil and coal. She would get a stock of coal in so she could supply people with half a hundredweight at a time. Or there was a Mr Stiff who came from Kersey with a horse-drawn van. That was a kind of general stores. You could get anything from him, oil included.'

Bower House Tye is a small cluster of dwellings that stands above the valley of the Box, about equally distant from the villages of Boxford to the west and Polstead to the south. It is just within the parish boundary of Polstead. In medieval times the fields that stretch up from the valley in long undulations to a height of not much more than two hundred feet were grazed by thousands of sheep. When George was born, they were cropped, as they are today, with wheat and barley, for this part of Suffolk is rolling arable land on the edge of what has become known as 'Constable' country.

George has spent all his life in the area of these two villages. They are quite unlike each other, although the same river flows through both. Polstead, apart from the steep street rising from near the ponds to the village green, scatters itself over the slopes of the valley. Boxford is compact with terraced streets mostly of Tudor houses. When George was a boy it had a collection of shops, crafts and trades which made it a natural centre for the surrounding farmsteads. Farming, and its related trades, was the main

11

occupation of the district. Even today farmers and farm workers together form the second largest group in the community.

George came of Suffolk stock. His father was born in the neighbouring parish of Edwardstone, but his mother, Betsy Jane Wollard, came from Burstall, a village further east and not far from Ipswich. He never knew his paternal grandfather. The man, however, was a farm worker like his son, and he died while eating his breakfast one morning, at harvest time, in a field on the outskirts of Boxford. But his maternal grandfather, George did know, and remembers him as a big man.

'He was very strict. He was a bit on the religious side, and - oh dear, you daren't do anything wrong, do you get a back-hander. I can remember that. He came to the Tye before I was born. A local farmer had a portable steam engine, and my grandfather came to drive that. I remember when he retired he lived next to Mr Richardson, the thatcher. I think he was eighty-three when he died, and just before he died, he'd walk all the way to Hadleigh Baptist Chapel on a Sunday morning, about six miles there and back.'

George's mother did not inherit her father's physique. She was a small woman like her own mother, with a strong nose and far-seeing eyes. She was quiet, kind-hearted and also 'a bit on the religious side' - a woman who bore the poverty and hardship of her life with a resignation that showed in the slightest down-turn of her mouth.

'She'd do anything for anyone, just as much as ever she could. I never heard her grumble, and if one of us was finding fault with somebody else, she would say, "You shouldn't do that. We've all got our own faults." I think she influenced me to do things for other people.

'We were a happy family. Well, we had to be. There was no sense getting excited or aggravated. You had to take things as they came. And my mother and father - they were very close.

'But sometimes they made me laugh. Sometimes on a Sunday morning - that nearly always happened on a Sunday morning - she'd get up and be a little bit . . . well, you know, you had to be careful what you said, otherwise she'd fly. Well, my father, sometimes he'd do it in a joke. He'd say something to her, and then she'd start a-jawing, and they'd have a little bit of a shindy. He'd have his breakfast. He wouldn't worry. He'd sort of laugh at her, and he'd say, "You're gettin' yourself into a fine trim

12

this mornin', in't yer mate?" I used to laugh at that. And he'd finish his breakfast, get up and say, "Well, I'll get outside for a little while, and 'haps you'll be better tempered when I come back." And that's all there was to it. And about five minutes after she'd go to the door and call him.

'Oh, she had cause enough for grumbling. I mean there wasn't a regular wage coming in every week. You couldn't keep a bob or two in your pocket in case anything happened. There was just enough to scrape through for the week, and that was hard. But, no, she didn't grumble. We couldn't go anywhere or do anything, like youngsters do today, but we were all happy enough, that we were.'

2
Schooldays

George's earliest memory is his first day at school. He started at the Easter term of 1897. He was a little over four years old and was one of nearly a hundred pupils attending the school at Polstead. It had been opened on October 9th 1876 as a board school, with parents having to pay a penny a week in fees, but by the time George attended, the Free Education Act had made it an elementary school.

It still stands, with high windows and high-pitched gables in Cock Lane, just off the village green, and is an example of the rather better kind of Victorian school building. There's a playground on one side and, at the back, is a field that slopes gently into the valley. (The school was closed in July 1990).

It is hardly surprising that George should remember his first day because, on arrival at the school, he was caned, albeit not too seriously. There were two ways of getting to school. One of them - straight down the road and then across fields and through Sprott's farmyard into Cock Lane - was almost two miles, and was the favoured route in dry weather. The other was a two-and-a-half mile walk by road across Polstead Heath.

The shorter route was taken on this first morning, and George was being looked after by his elder brother, Arthur, and a friend of his from next door. The two older boys had begun playing marbles in the road, and they were scarcely more than five minutes' walk away from home when they heard the sound of the school bell across the fields.

'They picked up the marbles, and Arthur got hold of one of my hands and his friend the other, and I was more or less dragged to school. I got the blame because they said they couldn't get me along. The headmaster, he showed me the cane, and he said, "I'll have to use this on you," and as he did so the cane sort of bent over and caught the back of my collar and split it. I can remember that. But I never felt it. It just hit my collar.'

The headmaster, throughout the whole of George's schooldays, was Mr T. H. Bromham, a distinguished-looking man of medium height with fair hair, a slightly drooping moustache, and glasses. He was a strict man, but George evidently got on very well with him. He was frequently picked out for the favoured jobs, although this invariably meant running errands or doing household chores.

There was 'a fair bit of caning at school in those days,' but then there were 'some really unruly boys, always in trouble'. He had the cane only once more during the whole of his schooling, and then he was about thirteen years old. It was hay-making time.

'We got playing about in the hayfield, and we hung about there so long that I said, "Well, we'll stop here now and go to school after dinner". Well, when we all turned up, Mr Bromham said, "Where'd you get to this morning together?" I told him that we'd been playing around in the hayfield and that it had got a bit late. "I suppose I shall have to take the blame," I said, "because they were ruled along o' me." So he gave me the cane across the backside. The others didn't get it. He just gave it to me, being as I was the oldest, and he said, "You'll have to take the blame." So I did. He could be cruel sometimes, with some of the boys.'

Mr Bromham was helped in the school by his wife, his sister, and one other young woman, May Howlett, who was six or seven years older than George. Apart from the morning prayer, which began the school day, most of the time was occupied in teaching reading, writing and arithmetic, although there was time for painting and drawing as well, but what George liked most of all was working on Mr Bromham's allotment.

The headmaster was clearly a practical man. Most of the boys he taught would end up working on a farm, and most would also have to know how to grow their own vegetables. So he gave them some practical experience, and got his own gardening done at the same time. He had two strips of land, and each of these he divided into four plots. He put two boys to work on each plot. Potatoes, peas, runner beans and broad beans, carrots, parsnips, beetroot, cabbages and sprouts, celery and onions were all grown on Mr Bromham's land.

'It taught us gardening, and that was very good. It was a good insight for young lads. Then, after school, I'd do a bit of gardening with my father. I used to love to get on the garden with him. I think that, more than anything else, was what made me

15

interested in growing things. He had us all working on the garden from time to time. He'd plant broad beans with his potatoes, not the early variety - Red Rose, I think it was - but with the main crop. He used to grow the old Majestic - that's still grown today - and Up-to-Date, but that's gone off the market. A pity - that was a nice potato. Then there was Sharp's Express, and a blue kidney potato that I think my father used to call Blue Fluke. That wasn't a prolific potato, but that had a lovely flavour. Well, he'd put up a line on a couple of sticks and dib the holes, and then I had to follow and put a potato in each hole and a broad bean with it. After the harvest was in, my father would perhaps have a day off from work, and that's when he'd take up his potatoes. And those beans - they came up nice at harvest time. Green Windsor and White Windsor they were - a nice big bean, although not as many in a pod as you get today.'

Another after-school job was to go round the lanes collecting horse manure.

'I had to do that at night with a trolley my father had made. If we hadn't got the trolley, then we had a bucket. We always had something to do. He used to say to me, "You don't want to play about. You've had enough of that at school." So all of us had some job to do. We expected it.

'That's how it was; we didn't have any games or pastimes in the home like the kids have today. There wasn't the money for that. There wouldn't have been the time anyway. Too many things to do.

'I don't think we had any books either to speak of. We didn't have time for reading - any of us. And I was never one to sit indoors. The only reading and playing we did was at school.'

Boys and girls were taught together in each class at Polstead, but at the midday break they sorted themselves out and seldom mixed.

'Our mothers used to make all our clothes. The boys wore little jackets and trousers. Some of them wore sailor suits. The trousers weren't as short as they are today. They came down to just below the knee, and then when we got near the school-leaving age, we went into long trousers. The girls wore little dresses of different colours, most of them with an apron on top. They looked quite nice. But today I see the children going to the village school, and they're dressed real nice - better than we had to be on a Sunday.

'I only had one real school pal - someone I liked better than anyone else. He was Reggie Coxsedge, the son of William Coxsedge, who used to have Polstead water mill. We were always in the same class, and sometimes I'd go down with him to dinner. He was a happy boy - that's what I liked about him. He never got into any trouble - always happy, always laughing. But I didn't see much of him after we left school, and he got killed in the first world war.

I didn't have any girl friends at school. Never thought about them.'

At midday there was a two-hour break, and this was mostly a time for play, but even that sometimes had a practical purpose, at least at hay-making time.

'We boys would get down to Polstead Park. I don't know what the girls did. They didn't come with us. Mr Daking had the hay there, and when that was cut he loved to see the children picking it up and throwing it about. That done it good, you see. Helped to make it. So he never told the children to keep off the park. He had a machine called a hay-shaker. That picked up the hay and scattered it. We liked to walk behind that. Used to get smothered with the hay. That let the sun into it, you see. And the more sun you had the quicker the hay was made. Then he had a horse-rake to rake it into rows. Then you cocked it, made heaps of it. That all helped to make the hay, and gave it that nice smell. That's a really lovely smell. I used to like that as a boy.'

Within the park at Polstead - once a deer park of the manor - stands the Hall. It is a building of fine eighteenth-century proportions masking an earlier Tudor dwelling. Nearby is the small Norman church, built in the middle of the twelfth century, with the only stone spire left in Suffolk. But it is the trees rather than the buildings that George remembers - the oaks and the chestnuts. One oak was reputed to be well over twelve hundred years old. This was the gospel oak, which stood between the church and the Hall, and was believed to be the site of some form of worship since Saxon times. It eventually fell in the winter of 1953, and self-seeded oaks now stand in its place.

Religious services round gospel oaks are invariably part of rogationtide ceremonies and the beating of bounds, but George remembers services round the Polstead oak as quite separate from the beating of bounds. They were held in July, and people made their way to the park on foot and in horse-drawn carts in their scores. There would be a local Salvation Army band or a band from Polstead Heath to play the hymns. There was a sense of occasion and perhaps a recognition of ancient and only half-understood ceremonies. They were, in George's words, 'nice services'.

Rather more memorable for him were the horse-chestnut trees, for these provided the source of one of the few games he played as a schoolboy - conkers. It was played then, as now, by threading a string through the horse-chestnut and taking it in turns with another boy to hit each other's conker until one was smashed. The secret of acquiring a champion conker was in the way it was hardened. Boys had all sorts of theories about how to do this, from soaking them in vinegar to baking them in the oven.

'I used to bring them home and dry them off. But if you baked them and they got too silly[1] hard, then they just split. I used to let them harden off near the fireplace, so they hardened off nice and steady.'

The school games that were played were football, cricket and, rather surprisingly for those times, pole vaulting. 'I could go over eight feet. We were all pretty good at that. I liked football, and I liked cricket, until one day when I was fielding, the ball shot forward and hit a molehill, and up that came and caught me in the mouth. I didn't like cricket after that. I said to myself, "I'm not a-goin' in for that again." And I didn't if I could help it.'

All the games were played in the field at the back of the school. It sloped down into the valley, so at football one side was always playing uphill. Marbles and leapfrog were the main unorganized games, and usually there were more important things to do. Having fun was not a priority in George's childhood.

At Bower House Tye George was the boy who was always ready to do the odd jobs that would earn a copper or two for his mother. It was George who did the errands for the neighbours. There was no milk delivery, so he had to collect the milk from neighbouring farms.

'I was up soon after six in the mornings, and sometimes I've gone to Kersey Uplands, or Hadleigh Heath or Polstead Heath. I fetched the milk in a can. Perhaps I'd get it for two or three people at the same time. I'd get back about eight o'clock, have a piece of food, and then be off to school. We had to be there by nine. There

1 Suffolk dialect, meaning excessively. It is quite usual to give a double emphasis, as George does here.

wasn't much to eat in those days. We was glad to get anything. We'd have a basin of hot water - hot-water soup we used to call it - bread soaked in hot water, and perhaps a piece of dripping put in just to make it a wee bit greasy. I've often had that to go to school on, after nearly two hours walking to get the milk. But there was nothing much you could get then. We hadn't got the money. Father got only ten bob (50p) a week. And if there was a wet day, then he lost a day's money. So it wasn't regular every week.'

The young Everett boy's willingness to help others was quickly noticed by his schoolmaster, and he was singled out for all sorts of domestic jobs. The schoolhouse was next door to the school.

'Sometimes he'd get me to go round to the door of the house to see the maid - Susan King was her name - and to get some kindling for her, or coke, or coal, or anything like that. Or perhaps I'd go and bang the mats. Well, afterwards, I'd get a bit of cake or something. So that was all right. Sometimes I used to go to Stoke [1] for him, shopping. And I've been down to Boxford shopping, too. Yes, I was rather a lucky young feller. I got on well with him.'

About the house George would give similar help to his mother, cleaning the oil lamps, or darning his own socks. But it was the paid jobs that were important as a way of supplementing the meagre financial resources of the household. Although the family qualified for parish relief, 'if you went to the parish, you'd only get about seven and sixpence (37$\frac{1}{2}$p). I remember there were two men used to come round, one collecting the rates - he was Charlie Day and lived at the Polstead Heath Shoulder o' Mutton - and then there was what they called the Relieving Officer. He had more than one parish to look after, 'tis true. You had to apply to him for help. Mr Lavender was his name. He used to cycle round, and he'd come and take full particulars of the family and how much money it had coming in. He was a jolly good feller. It didn't produce much, but you were glad of a couple of bob in those days. That was the reason I'd go out to earn a shilling for me mother. Same as harvest time. I didn't play around same as the other children. I liked to get down on the farm to get a shilling or two.

During harvest farmers were especially glad of child labour. They got the work done without the necessity of increasing the wages of their men. George was ten or eleven when he first lent

1 Stoke by Nayland is a mile and a half from the school and Boxford three miles away.

a hand in the harvest field. A neighbour, the publican Mr Fletcher at The Brewer's Arms, had about thirteen acres down to wheat and barley. All this corn was mown with a scythe, and some men from Boxford had come up to help get it in. It had to be tied by hand.

'Well, I'd go and make the bands[1] for them - for them to tie up the corn. I would go along, you see, and pull out a few ears, tie them together, and put them down for the men, so they could bind up the sheaves. Well, perhaps during the night I'd get about thre'pence (11/4p). That seemed a lot to me. I'd take it home and give it to mother. You did that for six days and it was eighteen pence (71/2p). Perhaps some of them would make it up to two bob (10p). Well, that was very good. That helped mother a lot.'

Although the sail-reaper was already in use, barley for malting was invariably cut with a scythe and was not always put into sheaves; it was frequently left loose. Arthur Young in his *General View of the Agriculture of the County of Suffolk* (1813) remarked, 'Barley is everywhere in Suffolk mown and left loose, the neater method of binding in sheaves is not practised.' Both Mr Fletcher's wheat and barley, however, were put into sheaves, and George was later allowed to make these himself, and the publican's son, Frank, made the binds by pulling out a few ears of corn and twisting them into a band. Mr Fletcher showed George how to gather the corn into a sheaf.

'But I wasn't man enough, you see, to gavel[2] up and hold it to make a full sheaf. I had to have two goes at it. You get hold of a piece and just put your foot on the bottom, so that help to hold it, and then you sort of slide that along and gavel it up till you can get what you can hold, and then you lay that down and go to the next piece.' (The sheaf would then be tied by Frank.) 'But as I got more of a man I got to do the lot in one go. If the wheat was long - as they used to grow wheat in those days, different from today - I would pull out a few ears, seven or eight of them, and I could do it with one hand, I didn't need a bind. You just get hold of the ears and put them under your sheaf, and then get hold of the straw and just twist that round underneath the ears. That was really hard work. I mean your poor old arms would get scratched. The

---

1 Suffolk dialect. Moor gives 'Binnd - a bind, anything to tie up a bundle with … or what shoves of wheat or beans are bound up with.'
2 Suffolk dialect. George is using the word simply to mean 'to gather', but its original meaning is to rake mown barley into rows ready to be pitched on to the wagon for carting. (Moor and Claxton).

blood was always running down.

'It was the same cutting round the hedges. You'd some-times get hold of a bramble or thistle. Well, some of the men, they'd cut the foot off an old stocking and put the leg part on their arms. But I don't know, I always fared to meddle with anything on my arms. That's why I rolled my sleeves up. Another thing - there were a lot of weeds at that time of day. They didn't have the sprays they have today. Well, you'd get perhaps a lot of mayweed, and that'd get in a cut, and then you'd get a little bit of a fester. That was hard old work for a boy.'

The next year, when George was eleven or twelve, he went to do odd jobs for a man who later was to become a regular employer - Mr Edward Lilley. He was what, in those days, would have been called, a big, fine man. He weighed fifteen or sixteen stone, worked hard, and expected everyone to do the same. He farmed 39 acres, and hired nearly a hundred more, at Brewery farm, close to George's home. He also brewed beer, and the barley grains that were thrown out were fed to the pigs. It was George's job to mix these in with their food. Sometimes there would be as many as a hundred pigs.

'They were black pigs - that was the Essex pig, I think. Then there were the Gloucester Spot - well, we used to call them plum puddings, brown and white they were.'

On Saturday George had his own duties about the home. Apart from the oil lamps, there were the boots, and the knives and forks to clean, and kindling to be chopped. Then the rest of the day was his own, and if he was not earning that copper or two on the farm, he still liked to get in the fields where the men were at work, and especially if they were using horses. 'I used to love to get among the horses.' Although he was never to become a fully-fledged horseman, George felt an early affinity with horses, which helped him to understand them, and proved of value to him in the only time that he has ever left Suffolk - during the Great War of 1914-18.

3
Stone Picking and Gleaning

There were two activities of the farming year which were essential to the hard-pressed economy of the farm-worker's household. They were stone picking and gleaning. Both were largely the responsibility of the mother and her children.

The Box valley is an area of London clay. It provides good agricultural land for the profitable corn crops, but it also provides a liberal crop of flints. Many generations have picked millions of stones from these fields, but they are still freckled with the white and metalled flash of innumerable flints.

Although they are no longer picked, the corn yield is greater than ever. Admittedly farmers have the benefit of better strains of wheat and barley, modern fertilisers and other agricultural aids, but even at the turn of the eighteenth century that great agriculturalist, Arthur Young, carried out an experiment on the other side of Suffolk which showed that the yield from fields which had been left untouched was greater than that from the stone-picked land.

There was, however, another reason for stone picking. It provided, before the motor car required a better surface, the material for road making. Originally, individual parishes were responsible for the upkeep of their own roads, but by the time George was a boy, the county council had taken on the responsibility! This, however, did not alter the demand for flints, because the same method of road making continued, and the same men did the work.

Stone picking for George was an evening job, and was done usually towards the end of March.

'When we came home from school we had to go stone picking - us children, and often mother too. We had to pick twenty-four bushels for half-a-crown (12 1/2p).

1 The Local Government Act 1888 transferred the responsibility to the county authority.

22

'We used to come home from school, have a cup of tea, and then we had to go into the field, and we'd be picking them up till you couldn't see any longer. We did that every year.

'Of course that all depended how thick they laid how much you got, but I suppose you could say that, if they laid pretty fair, two or three of you could pick up five or six bushels a night. We always did it in the spring before the corn got too high. If that got too high you couldn't find them. And a little bit of treading the young corn was reckoned to be good for it.

'We used to have peck measures. That was a bag tied round us like an apron. We put the stones into that, and when it was full we'd shoot them out into a heap. When we'd done that four times that was a bushel, and then we'd put a little tally stone into a hollow in the earth. That's how we used to count the bushels. I don't think anyone tried to diddle the tally, leastways I didn't. I was very particular about that. My mother and my father always said, "You give a proper measure, you know. No mucking about." And I always did. We piled the stones into eight bushel heaps.'

In any event, there wasn't much opportunity to cheat the farmer. He would measure out the first load he collected from the field, and then mark the height of the load on the inside of the tumbril with a piece of chalk.

Sometimes the farmer would dump the stones in large heaps in a corner of the field, but on other occasions he would take them immediately out onto the road and dump them on the verge at a spot previously arranged with the roadmen. Road making, in the days before tarmacadam, was a winter occupation. The flints were rolled out on to the cart-tracked surface, and the roadmen had to break them down.

'I remember there were two roadmen at Polstead. They had hammers, and they'd go along and crack all the big flints. That was hard work, and bits of flint would fly about in a dangerous way. Then a steam-roller would come along and roll them out. That was followed by the water tank. The watered flints would be rolled again, and then left for the traffic to grind in the rest. And of course they were all horse-drawn carts with iron-rimmed wheels in those days.'

On fields of spring-drilled corn, the earth would have been disturbed sufficiently to bring many of the stones to the surface, but on winter-sown land the earth would have hardened and buried the flints. Then the farmer would run a harrow over these

23

fields to loosen the stones. Often four nights' work would be enough to earn half-a-crown and that, after all, was a quarter of the father's wage.

'There was nothing else to it. You wouldn't get youngsters doing it these days, but we never thought about it. That didn't do us any harm. You'd do anything to get a bob or two, and mother was glad of that.'

It was stone-picking money, earned at night, that, some years later, paid for George's first suit.

'That was what was called a Norfolk suit. It was grey and had straps down the front and a belt round it. Oh they were good suits, with good big pockets. I was about fourteen, and I was proud of that suit. Oh, I was absolutely It when I'd got that on. I think I wore it when I went to the children's anniversary at Polstead Heath Chapel. I don't know how much it cost, but it came out of the stone-picking money, I know that. That were a fine suit, and I think we looked better then than some teenagers do today. I don't like it myself, the way they go about - these leather jackets, and one thing and another. They look proper scruffy.'

Almost as important as stone picking to the household economy were the results of gleaning - gathering the remnants of corn left in the field after harvest. This didn't produce money, but it did provide flour for making bread.

The more primitive the method of cutting the corn the greater the yield for the gleaners. The scythe, which had long ago succeeded the sickle, had mostly been replaced by either the clipper or the sail-reaper. The clipper, which was a modification of the grass mower and was sometimes known as a rack-engine, and the sail-reaper, which were both drawn by horses, were more productive for the gleaners than the reaper and binder that succeeded them.

No one was allowed into the fields for gleaning until the farmer was satisfied with his own harvesting of the crop. If there was still some corn to be raked up, the farmer left a single shock (they are never called stocks in Suffolk) remaining in the field. This was universally known as 'the policeman'. When the shock was removed it was a sign that the gleaners could move in. In earlier times it was the custom, in some villages, to ring the church bell as a sign that gleaning could begin.

Some farmers would leave 'the policeman' there as long as possible while their men raked and re-raked the field.

Over-anxious gleaners were sometimes said to remove 'the police-man' at night, but George's parents weren't among them. 'Some could have done it, but I know we never did.'

The school holidays coincided with harvesting, so that children were always on hand for gleaning. George was usually accompanied by one of his brothers and his elder sister, Ruth. She made a practice of getting out as early in the morning as she could. She would take something to eat with her and would not trouble to return home until the evening.

'The ordinary clipper was a machine that took about a four-foot cut. The man sitting on it had a rake, just to gavel the corn and hold it on to the lattice at the side of the machine. Then when there was enough to make a sheaf, he just pressed that down and it dropped onto the ground. The sheaves were tied up by hand by the workers in the harvest field, and then put in traves[1]. Well, with a machine like that you used to get more loose wheat dropping about on the field. When the binder come in that was more clean. They had what we called a dew rake. That was drawn by a horse and was raked through the stubbles to gather up the remaining corn. And that was left in rows about fifty yards apart. Well, we used to watch for that, you see, because when you went gleaning there was always more to pick up where the rows had been. Often you'd get more short ears, some that had been clipped off.

'Well, three or four of us would go gleaning, and if father wanted the straw, we would gavel up the corn and tie it in bunches, straw and all. But if he didn't want the straw, we'd cut the heads off and put them in a bag. We got enough one year, when it was threshed and sent to the mill, for half a sack of flour. There was one man who always took it to the mill for all the gleaners. Well, that flour came as a great help. Mother used it for making bread. So I reckon gleaning was better than running and playing about.

'When the binder started coming out, there weren't so much for the people to pick up. So gradually they forgot it and gleaning died out. You didn't see so much of it after the first world war at any rate.'

But some gleaning - and stone picking too - continued in this part of Suffolk into the nineteen-twenties.

The flour that resulted from gleaning was nowhere near enough to last for a year's bread-making. So often farmers would

1 Suffolk dialect: shocks of corn

allow their workers a portion of wheat as one of the perquisites of working on the farm for no more than a few shillings a week. But the practice was not universal, and it was not one from which the Everett family benefited. So flour had frequently to be bought.

'There was a man living on the Tye who sold coal and flour, and mother bought flour from him. He got it from Raydon Mill, but that's not working now.'

The two-up and two-down cottage at the Tye had its own brick oven, the roof of which was an arch of skilfully laid bricks. Mrs Everett did her baking once a week. In George's childhood bread was unquestionably the most important ingredient in the family's diet. Meat, except for the occasional rabbit caught with the farmer's permission, was hard to come by, and there was no communal pig-keeping by groups of workers. They couldn't afford it. But the flour was good, coarse stone-ground whole-wheat.

Yeast was easily obtained, and was also necessary for brewing beer. It was often kept over from the brewing to be used for bread-making. Providing it was coolly stored it would keep for several months.

'The oven was heated by wood - faggots and any other wood father could get hold of and mother would handle - but not thorn or anything like that, though chance time they had a bit or two of thorn go in just to help.'

The wood was thrown into the oven or pushed in with a fork on a long handle, set light to, and the door slammed shut, the smoke escaping through the chimney by the oven door. The wood had to burn until only the ash was left and the bricks were glowing red hot. Meanwhile Mrs Everett had placed the dough in a covered earthenware bowl near the oven, but not too near, because it should not be too warm for the dough to rise. After it had risen it was kneaded again and put into baking tins and left to rise again before being placed in the oven. First, however, the ash had to be scraped out. Both this operation and placing the tins of dough inside had to be done very quickly, so that as little heat as possible escaped while the door was open.

'The bread would take about an hour to bake, and mother used to bake other things at the same time, like short cakes. The bread was lovely. That somehow tasted different from what it does today.'

There are no brick ovens in use at Bower House Tye or at

Boxford today, but there is organically grown wheat which is stone-ground into wholewheat flour, and there are still some local women, and perhaps rather more young wives of newcomers to the village, who bake their own bread, albeit in modern electric ovens.

4
Old Remedies

The bread that tasted different, because it was so much more nutritious than modern bread, was probably one of the reasons why there was comparatively little illness in the Everett household. They could not afford to be ill. A cold was never something that warranted calling Dr Thompson - 'a fine sort of man, tall, biggish, about fourteen or fifteen stone. He was a very nice man, a bit stern, but pretty good. He died, I think, during the first world war.' Colds were to be borne and mostly ignored.

'But when we did sometimes have terrible colds, mother would make a drink of home-made blackcurrant jam. That was like a syrup, and when you had that, that really did you good. There was one other little complaint that we got; that was called nettle rash. When that happened, mother would go out into the lane and gather the white nettle. She'd boil that and make what they call nettle tea. You had a spoonful or two of that, and that do get rid of the old nettle rash.

'But we were mostly all right. There was seldom anyone at home from school. Perhaps one of us *would* get the measles. That do come round now and again. I had it and so did my brother, Morris, who was killed in the first war. Apart from that we none of us had much wrong with us. There was whooping cough chance times, but I didn't get that. I have heard of some strange remedies for that, like putting a live dab on the chest and leaving it there 'till it dies, or passing the ill child through a slit in the trunk of a young ash tree. But the best-known cure was to eat a fried mouse, but mother never went along with that. There was some sort of liquorice she used to buy, and she'd make a drink out of that. It tasted very much like lozenges.

'They used to say that if you put your left sock on first, and your left trouser-leg before your right, that would cure the toothache. And there were lots of ways that were supposed to get rid of warts, like putting the froth of new beer on them three days

28

in a row and letting it dry off, or rubbing a green sloe on your warts and then throwing it over your left shoulder. I reckon these things were mostly superstitions more than cures, and anyway they'd already mostly gone when I was a boy, but I have heard it said that they'd put cobwebs on a cut, and of course you always put dock leaves on a nettle sting - that was well-known.

'I doubt that was for the whooping cough, but I remember when I was a lad there was a boy who would always eat mice. David Hughes was his name. I was still at school, and he was older than me. After school I would sometimes go down to the stack yard when they were threshing. Sometimes when you pick up a couple of sheaves from the stack you'd see a mouse or two under them. Well, he'd knock one on the head as they came off the stack, he would. Then he'd cut the head off, hold it up by the tail, and eat it fur and all. He'd eat the lot. I never fancied that myself.'

George has a vivid memory from the age of nine or ten of a cure for an epileptic fit, although it does not appear to have been tested at the time. He had walked down the hill to Boxford on one of his many errands, this time to call at the doctor's on behalf of one of the old people living at Bower House Tye. He stopped on the corner by the baker's shop (now a private house named The Old Bakery). Opposite is The White Hart, a timber-framed building with two pleasing front gables, dating from the sixteenth to seventeenth century. There is a forecourt and a large yard at the side. Close by the pub, on the river bank, grow the box trees from which the village acquired its name, but George's attention had been caught by the landlord, who was unfortunately subject to fits 'that would take two or three men to hold him down'.

'Well, he was in one of these fits, and I was agin the baker's shop. I stood a-lookin' in at The White Hart yard and was wondering what was going on. There was an old Gipsy woman beside me, and she asked, "What's wrong with that man?" So I replied, "Well, they tell me he do have terrible fits." "Oh," she say, "he can be cured of that quick. Take his shoe off," she say, "and let him smell inside of that. That'll cure him." I thought, "That's a funny thing," and I've remembered it ever since.

'Of course it was all dirt and dust in the middle of the village then. The road was made of rolled stones, and there was a lot of dust from that, and the kerbs of the pavements were made of round dark bricks. All the traffic was horses and carts, and if anyone came down with a load of barley for Mr Kemball's maltings, they'd go into The White Hart and tie up their horses and wagons in the yard.'

George never saw that Gipsy again, but when he was a boy there was another old woman who lived close by at Bower House Tye who was reputed to be a witch. It is more than likely that the reputation was the result of superstition and malicious gossip because George has no recollection of any acts of either good or evil attributed to her.

'But I remember she was a funny old girl. I can picture her now. She used to wear a little straw bonnet and a black skirt and shawl. But so did a lot of women. At that time of day they nearly all seemed to dress alike. A lot of them would wear a veil too. If she *was* a witch, I didn't know anything about it, but there was gossip, you understand. And no-one would rile her. But that was said that if you put a knife under your doormat the witch wouldn't come in. The house she lived in was right opposite Mr Lilley's farm. It had a nice little garden full of greengage trees, but that's all gone now.'

George was only about eight or nine when he faced, for the first time, the finality of death. There was a man missing - everyone was talking about it. Another young lad, about a year older than me, said, "Shall we go out and look for him?" I said, "Yes, we'll go." And we did. Naturally enough we took the route towards the school that we knew best; that go through the yard of Sprott's Farm, and right by the yard is Dollop's Wood. Just as we were a-goin' into the wood, we saw a policeman standing there. He say, "Where are you two lads off to then?" I said, "We're a-lookin' for Mr Strutt." "Well, I don't think you're man enough to look for him," he say. "We'll find him. Do you go back." Well, apparently they'd just found him. He'd hung himself in the wood. I thought at the time that was a funny thing to do. I couldn't understand it at all. I couldn't see why anyone should want to do that.'

The walk between school and home, however, was normally far less eventful and, it seems, invariably pleasurable and sometimes even financially rewarding. It was on this daily walk that the boy George first absorbed the scents, sounds and scenes of the countryside, learned, without being aware of learning, the names of the wild flowers and the birds, and saw how the farming year was ordered. He already had his favourite tree. It was the poplar, and the reason for his choice: 'Because they grew high into the sky, and they looked nice.' There was, however, another reason: they provided the chance for some schoolboy sport.

Polstead derives its name from 'a place of pools', and in George's boyhood two large ponds were divided by a roadway that led to a farm. Opposite is a bridge which has to be crossed to reach the village.

'As boys we used to stand over on the bridge, and there were three or four poplar trees on the far side of the pond, and we had to see who could throw stones over the top of them. That was our aim. That was quite a long throw, but we could get them up and just get them over, and they'd fall into the next pond. Perhaps that's why I liked the poplar, but I like the horse chestnut too, and that gave us a lot of sport with conkers. But the ash, I never have liked that. You can't get anything to grow near an ash tree, that you can't.'

The possibility of financial reward on the walk home from school arose usually during the spring. The Rector of Polstead, the Reverend Francis Eld, would often take a walk at that time of the year.

'He'd got a horse and carriage, and he had a groom who used to drive him around, but in the spring he'd very often walk up to the Tye to visit one or two people, and he most always had a pocketful of coppers. When he was a-comin' back he usually met us on the way from school, and he'd stop and have a tale with us, and then he'd put his hand in his pocket and throw up a handful of coppers for us to pick up.

'One afternoon, just as the birds were layin', there was a blackbird on a holly stub. That sit there on the nest, and that was such a beautiful shoot. I got me catapult, and just took aim, and I cut it off there where it sit. I was vexed afterwards when I thought about it. And just as we left and were comin' round Dollop's Wood, the Reverend came along too. If he'd a-been a minute sooner he would have seen me do that. I shouldn't have got no coppers then. I might have got a clip of the ear or something.'

Later in his life George was to use the catapult to kill for the pot, but the killing of the blackbird was uncharacteristic of a boy who was essentially kind by nature and who was to grow into a gentle though practical man. He never, for example, like many boys of his age, collected birds eggs, except for the eggs of the sparrow, and this was only because the sparrow population was so high that they were a menace to farmers.

'I used to get the sparrows' eggs out of the stacks and thatched buildings round the farmyard. I never liked it much because in a thatched roof there could always be a rat if you put your hand in. So I'd be a little bit dubious on that job.'

The Suffolk man is indeed wary, but wary from experience and because of a native common sense. That quality George learned early in his life.

5
The End of School

In George's boyhood the farm was dependent upon the horse, not only for ploughing and drilling and reaping, but for carting and other innumerable jobs. There could have been no husbandry without horses, and consequently great care was lavished upon them. Later in his life George both cared for horses and ploughed with them. The two activities would traditionally have qualified him for the job of a horseman, but he rejected this as a potential threat to his independence. Nevertheless from his schooldays he became familiar with horses and their ways.

The horse his father had tripped over on the night of George's birth brought the boy home from school on many occasions. It was a dark bay, a big animal, long in the body and inappropriately called 'Short'.

'At the time I was going to school, Mr Daking had Polstead Ponds Farm and Bower House Farm, and at haymaking time they used to borrow that old horse and take him down to Polstead. He was such a quiet old feller.

'Well, when they'd done with him in the afternoon, they'd put him on the road and say, "You can go home," and off he'd go home to Bower House Farm. I got to know that, because on haymaking days we'd go from the school down on to the park, and I'd think to myself, "I can have a ride home tonight". So I would cut across Sprott's Farm, up the path, and meet the old horse on his way home. I'd pull him alongside the bank, jump on his back, and then we'd be off home together. Oh yes, I remember that old horse well, quiet and gentle he was.

'But at all times of the year I liked to get on the farm and have a ride on the horses. When the men were in the field a-ploughing, I'd be there, doing something or other. Then when they took off about three o'clock to go home, I'd have a ride on one of the horses. Then at harvest they would have a trace horse to help take the corn out of the field, and I would always ride that horse if I could.

33

'I remember one harvest especially. That would be a Monday morning, because on the Saturday previous that happened to be a damp day and they couldn't do much harvesting, so they called it off that day. Well, there was a circus on at Hadleigh, and I'd never been to a circus. My father said, "Come you along, and we'll go to the circus." So we did. Well, they had some clowns that stood on the horses and rode round the ring. That looked easy enough to me, and I thought to myself, "I'll have a go at that".

'Well, on the Monday, that was a nice morning and they started harvesting again. Mr Daking came up from Polstead Ponds to Bower House, and he called me and said, "Come on, we're a-goin' to cart the wheat today". So I went along with him and had a ride on the trace horse.

'When I got off the cart road and on to the field - that was a fourteen-acre field - to go across to where they were loading the wheat, I thought to myself, "Well, I'm goin' to see if I can stand on this horse". And I did. I stood up on that old horse - a strawberry roan called Duke, although it was a mare - and she was soon trotting away. Mr Daking, he daren't speak until I got to the far end. Then he said, "I think you've done very well, but I want you to sit on there. I don't want you to stand".

'Well, when we got back to the farm, where my father was working at the stack with the stacker, he said, "Dick, did you know you've got a circus man with you?"

'My father said, "What do you mean?" Then he asked if we'd been to the circus on Saturday night, and told my father how I'd been riding the horse a-standing on its back. As luck would have it she was a nice broad mare, and I'd watched where the clowns stood, right on the back part. So I did the same. But that didn't make me feel I wanted to join the circus. Oh no, I just liked the circus, that's all. There was Robert Fossett's, I remember. They had a rider that had baskets put on his feet and then he was blindfolded, but he still run across the ring and jump on his horse. He was a clever feller.'

There were few of the activities of the farm with which George did not become familiar during his schooldays, and sometimes the need to earn those extra coppers to help the hard-pressed family budget meant depriving himself of childhood pleasures. Not that this seemed to worry him. It was accepted as necessary without any sense of deprivation, and even enjoyed. If you've got to do something you might as well enjoy it was

George's philosophy, even as a boy.

The Methodist Chapel at Polstead Heath, about a mile from George's home, and the Baptist Chapel at Hadleigh Heath, also about a mile away, were the centres of religious life for the Everett household. Mrs Everett was punctilious in her attendance. When George first began going regularly to Sunday school, he walked to Hadleigh Heath, but when he was a little older he made the three-mile walk to the Baptist Chapel at Hadleigh town, and walked the three miles back. By the time he was twelve, however, he was going every week to Sunday school at the Methodist Chapel at Polstead Heath. This seemed to be only a matter of family preference, although Betsy Everett was a Baptist by upbringing.

The chapel anniversaries were events in which the children were expected to take part, invariably by learning and reciting some poetry, usually of a sacred kind. George remembers, 'One year I had to learn two - one for the afternoon and one for the evening - but I'm blessed if I know what they were now.'

In the middle of the following week, usually a Wednesday, there would be a chapel social and outdoor sports. Polstead is renowned for its cherries, although today only one orchard remains. The local variety was known as Polstead Black. An old account remarks of it, 'The ripe fruit is black and of a refined and exceptional flavour which no one has succeeded in reproducing elsewhere'.

The chapel socials - or school treats, as they were known - were always in the summer at cherry-picking time.

'We used to have a nice fill of cherries, that we did. And there'd be races, and a band on Polstead Heath. Father and Mother would come, and I enjoyed that. But one year I had to miss it. I wanted to earn a little extra money. I had to go and single mangolds. The men would chop the mangolds out during the day, and perhaps they'd leave two or three together, and we had to single them out. This particular year that was my turn, and I thought to myself, "Well, I'll have to miss the treat". I could hear the band, and it was a lovely evening. I was about three-quarters of a mile away as the bird flies, and I could hear the children laughing. I thought to myself, "Well, blimey, I'm here, and there they are enjoying themselves". But I was earning money.

'I used to get a penny a row. The row would be about a hundred and sixty yards long. Of course some men would leave the mangolds a little bit thicker than others, and some would leave them practically single. So that varied how many rows you could do, but I would do about six of an evening. So that was sixpence I earned. And the next year I got thre'pence-ha'penny a row. And that's how I'd earn an extra penny or two. Well, I'd rather do that than be playing about. And Mother could always do with an extra copper.'

In spite of the fact that George spent most of his spare time and much of his school time either running errands or doing odd jobs to earn a few pence, he proved to be a clever if unambitious pupil.

He called himself 'jobbing boy' at school, because of the number of odd jobs he did. In the winter it was his task to get a scuttle of coke from the shed at the back of the school to feed two old French stoves, which were used to heat the school room. But nothing seemed to worry or disturb him, whether he was called upon suddenly to go shopping for the headmaster or to do his sums.

'I think working on the allotment was what I liked best about school. But I'd always take things as they came along. I'd listen to each lesson, and then do my best. Well, when I got into class seven, Mr Bromham held a special examination. I know I had to write an essay but I can't remember what that was about. Anyhow, three of us passed, and he called us X-Seven. We were in that class for two years - doing lessons similar to the others, except the sums were more difficult. Anyhow, I never had any trouble. At the end of it, he would have liked me to be a teacher. But I don't think I would have liked that.

'Well, my father said, "No, you can't be a teacher, boy. I want you out earning a bob or two." So I told the schoolmaster, "I'd like to get to work. I don't really want to be a teacher," I said. Well, I mean, I don't suppose there was a lot of money attached to it at that time of day.'

So a career in teaching, which was evidently thought a possibility by Mr Bromham, was never seriously entertained. There were more important considerations. If George really had momentarily thought about the likelihood of becoming a teacher, he quickly dismissed the idea. He already had a practical mind, and had accepted the inevitability of following his father on to the land. So he left school at Christmas 1906, a week or so before his fourteenth birthday.

6
His First Job

George started working for Mr Edward Lilley at Brewery Farm, Polstead, on January 1st 1907, the day he became fourteen. He had already done occasional jobs about the farm on Saturdays, and regarded himself as partly trained for day work.

Lilley then farmed a little less than a hundred acres, thirty-nine of them at Brewery Farm. The farmhouse was a small timber-framed and plastered Tudor building with a thatched roof. It still stands, although it has been sliced away from arable fields by a new road that by-passes the village of Boxford. The house had a cellar and a brewery, and Mr Lilley spent much of his time brewing and selling beer, leaving the farm to the five men he employed.

George's brother, Jack, was already working there as the milkman. 'First of all he worked for a thatcher at Polstead Heath, but after a year or two he left and came to Mr Lilley.' Most of Jack's time, however, was spent working in the brewery, although racking the beer was left to the boss. George described Mr Lilley as a big and fine man - a hard worker and a tough task-master. As a result he made a good living from his farm and his brewery.

George began that first day with his father's advice fresh in his mind. 'He really laid down the law for me. "Don't you ever put your hands on to anything that don't belong to you," he said. "If there's anything you want, you ask for it. He can only say yes or no. Don't you ever bring anything home, do you'll know all about it." And that's a thing I never did. I'd rather starve than pinch anything. If I wanted a swede - because, I mean, that was common food in those days - I would have to ask the boss if I could have one to take home. Or perhaps a white turnip. Some would let the white turnips run, and they'd have the tops. But if you wanted something like that, you just asked him, and he'd say, "Yes, you can take a few but don't take too many". And that's how I used to work it. But I never laid my hands on anything.'

That fourteenth birthday had one thing in common with the

day of his birth - the ground was covered with snow. The first job he did on the farm was filling snow - that is to say, carting it away from the front of the farmhouse, the driveway and the farmyard. It was lying two feet thick, and it was tiring work to shift it - a hard way to celebrate, but then birthdays didn't mean a great deal in his family, and his own was too close to Christmas to be regularly noticed. He was invariably reminded that he'd had his present at Christmas time.

Any odd jobs that needed doing fell to George's hands. He had to help his brother, Jack, mix the food for the cattle, and then help to feed them. Sometimes, if Jack was busy washing out casks in the brewery, the boy did the feeding himself. For all this he was paid half-a-crown (12 1/2p) a week.

Within four months he had got himself a rise. George soon found that he was expected to go to the farm twice on Sundays to feed the cattle, and he considered this was worth an additional sixpence (2 1/2p). 'But I had to tell a bit of a story to get it. I told him I'd got another job I could go to where I could earn three bob a week. And that's how I got another sixpence in the April.'

George demonstrated the same independence of spirit when, in the first year, he was helping to harvest a field of beans.

'Lilley liked to have them pulled off the stalks, but blast, that was punishing to the hands. So I used a rip[1] to cut down the whole stalk. When Mr Lilley came along and saw me doing it, he say, "What d'you think you're doing? You should be pulling them off." "Well, I in't a doin' that," I told him. "I'm doin' it like this." So he hollered at me, and I threw the hook at him. "I'm bloody well doin' it like this or I'm not doin' it at all." And I went on harvesting the beans with the rip. He just had to accept it.'

Pea harvesting was also a job which George enjoyed as a boy even before he was fully employed.

'By four o'clock in the morning I've often been down on the field picking with my father. He'd pick a few bags before he went to work . Each bag held forty pounds, and we were paid sixpence a bag. We used to like that job. But you had to be up early . You see, the earlier you picked the peas the quicker it was to get forty pounds, because they were just that little bit heavier before the sun come up.

---

1 A bill hook. Not given in this context by Moor, Forby or Claxton, but still widely used in this part of Suffolk.

'We used to harvest peas with a *pease-make*.[1] That were a straight handle, like a hoe handle and about the same length, with a blade just over a foot long at the end - a straight blade very slightly curved towards the tip.

'You had to get the peas at the bottom, near the ground. Then when you'd cut out a nice lot, you could just tip them over. Some chaps would cut them with a scythe.[2] Well, that was all right if the peas were standing up. You could often do it if there were poppies among the peas, because that would help them to stand up. But if they weren't standing - and sometimes you'd get some rain, and down they'd go, lying on top of one another - why then, that's when you had to harvest them with a pease-make.

'We'd wisp them up into heaps, and then leave them. They lay light then, and the sun would get into them, because they had to be fairly ripe - not silly ripe, mind you, but fairly ripe.

'After a few days we'd turn them over, give them another day or two, and then it was time to cart them. And you'd be surprised when you went to pick them up. They seemed as light as anything.

'They didn't always thresh them out in the fields. Sometimes they would, but as a rule we had to stack them, and then thresh them later. That separated the peas from the pods, and the pea straw - if the season was right - some of the farmers would cut up and give to the cattle, and to sheep especially. They reckoned it was good for sheep, and they loved it. But, of course, if that were a wet season, then the straw went rotten.

'The peas were fed to cattle, and to pigs as a rule. None of these peas was sent to market. They were dun peas or field peas, not for us to eat. But some farmers would grow what we called a maple pea - some people called them partridge peas. They were a dark pea with a faint stripe. They weren't as big as the field peas, but we were told that the miners used to eat them. They made more to the sack. But all the peas we grew were for cattle feed.

'Before the harvest, of course, there was the haymaking. The hay was cut by machine in June. Mr Lilley's head horseman did it with a grass-mower. Then that had to be turned over by hand rake. That were a wooden rake, and a whole gang of us would take a row each and pull it over. Then when that was ready

---

1 The implement is invariably referred to as a pea-make or pay-make, but as Forby notes, 'In Suffolk the instrument is always called a *pease-make*'.

2 Arthur Young describes a *pease-make* as 'the half of an old scythe fixed in a handle', and that may have been its origin, but there is no doubt that it became a purpose-made implement.

we used to rake it into rows and cock it.

'Then, if he wanted it for seed, we'd leave the grass to sprout again, and cut it in September or October. If he didn't want it for seed, then we'd feed it off with sheep.'

Now that George had left school and was working full-time on the farm he was, in accordance with custom, known as a lad. Lads were paid more than boys, who were still at school and recruited to help with the harvest and so keep the farmer's costs down. A lad at harvest time was treated and paid as a half-man. George got ten shillings (50p) a week at harvest time. He had to be at the stack when the loaded wagons were brought into the yard.

'But I couldn't unload the wagons on to the stack unless that was downhill' - that is to say, the stack building had not reached the height of the loaded wagon - 'then I could throw the sheaves down on to the stack. But when the stack was bigger I used to be up there and give the sheaves to the stacker from the man who was unloading them from the wagon.

'When I got a bit older I could go into the field, and then I'd do the loading. I don't say I could for wheat, but for oats and barley, I could pitch them on to the load. When you pick up a sheaf with a two-tine fork, you put the fork under it and just twist it a wee bit, and then you pick another one up, so you've got the two with the ear ends together. You have to do that, and then the man on the wagon puts his arms round it and keep it as you give it to him. So that look a bit like a sheaf untied, if you know what I mean, but it was important to twist them, so that one sheaf lapped over the other, with the ears inwards. That way you got two lots up on one forkful. So then I could take my turn, sometimes pitching, sometimes loading. I was only a half-man then.'

Traditionally not even a three-quarter man - a lad getting three-quarters of a man's pay - would be expected to do the pitching, which was the heaviest job at harvest time. He would normally be on top of the load, so that he could help with the stacking, the job which George had done as a half-man. He became a three-quarter man when he was eighteen.

'That was the year - 1911 it was - I got a full man's wages. If ever you asked for a rise Mr Lilley nearly had a fit. But at hay-making time I thought I'd have another go at him. I thought to myself, "I'm eighteen and, with the work I do, if I'm not worth a man's money, I'm going to pack it up." So I asked for two shillings rise. Cor blimey, he nearly went sky high. But I got it, and that made nine bob (45p) a week.'

At this time a farmer often wouldn't pay a man full-man's money until he could carry a sack of wheat across his shoulders. 'A sack of wheat was two hundredweight and two stone - eighteen stone. They didn't think you were worth man's money until you could do that. Well, I could manage it on my back, but when I was eighteen I didn't attempt to take it across my shoulders. I could manage a sack of oats or barley, but not wheat, nor peas, nor clover seed. That came out at twenty stone a sack. I'd carry them all on my back but not across my shouldres. Still, I told him that I did as much as any man he'd got and I was worth full-man's money.

'Then, when we took the harvest, he said, "Well, there'll be eight men and three-quarters." I said, "Who's the three-quarters?" He said, "Well, you are, of course." So I said, "You can cut me out of it. If I don't come in as a full man, I don't come in at all." So he turned to the others, and asked them what they had to say about it, and they said, "Let him come in." And so I got full-man's harvest.

'During that harvest I went up to Hightrees (a neighbouring farm). My brother had just finished and I went up there to borrow his scythe. We'd got another field of barley to cut.

'Well, I met the old chap, Mr Lilley, on the corner. We had a bit of a row because I didn't go to help look after the stock on the Sunday.

"Oh," I said, "I did it twice. I did it for my brother and I did it for your son, because he wanted to go to Bildeston to see his young lady. It was his turn Sunday, so you blame him not me." He said, "I went down there six o'clock last night and they hadn't been fed." I said, "Well, do you blame your son."

'Well, he put his fist over my nose. I drew back, and I took the scythe off my shoulder and I put it round the back of his legs. Ah, I'm not a-goin' to say what I said to him, but I reckon I scared him. We had a proper shindy, and I told him, "When I've done harvest, I'm finished. I can go into the army and get seven bob a week, my food and my clothes, and while I work on the land I shan't have anything." So I got men's money. I think that had risen from 12 to 13 shillings (65p) a week then. So I gained about six shillings (30p) that year, and that come in very useful, I can tell you.'

By this time the Everett family had moved down the hill from Bower House Tye into the village of Boxford, where George has remained ever since. The move had, in fact, been accomplished two years earlier, in 1909, but it was to be another nine years before his parents moved to the cottage he was to occupy until he was in his 88th year.

Always before harvest began there was the bargaining ceremony called 'taking the harvest'. It was the term traditionally used to describe the contract agreed between the workers and the farmer for getting the harvest in. Even in the early years of the present century the prospect of harvest dominated the life of the rural community. It was still, as it had been for centuries, the culmination of the year's life and work. Today, with so few men working on farms, it passes with little or no significance for most people living in the village.

Crops had been harvested from these lands for hundreds of years, and George was aware of this continuity as it reached the climax of harvest.

'That was all the year's work and so many lives depended on it. We had the Lord of the Harvest. He was the horseman. We used to call him the Lord, and he was the one who had to strike the bargain with Mr Lilley to get in the harvest for so much per man. We'd do it for six pounds a man, and that would be to do it in a month. If it took longer - well, you got no more money. But if you did it within the month, then you were getting more than your normal pay. He would give us a shilling each when we took the harvest. That was to bind[1] you. And we'd get an allowance of two bushels of malt each.'

Sometimes these contracts between the men and the farmer were written agreements, but Mr Lilley and his men were content to accept each others' word and the binding effect of a shilling.

It was the Lord of the Harvest [2] - the head horseman on Mr Lilley's farm - who led the team of mowers when they went to cut the barley with a scythe. It was he who set the rhythm and

1   W and H Rainbird in *On the Agriculture of Suffolk* (1849) record that the evening before the wheat harvest the men 'wet the sickle' - namely, took an allowance of beer. This was often drunk at the pub, 'and is the amount given by the farmer as earnest when hired for the harvest (generally one shilling a man) and as much more as they liked to spend.'

2   Claxton records that the title Lord of the Harvest was still used in the Needham Market district of Suffolk as late as 1930.

pace for the other reapers. The man immediately next to him was known as The Lady.

'Mowing barley, you just cut yourself into the field and then cut straight across it. You have to sweep it away from the standing corn, otherwise you couldn't get along. Well, there'd be six of us doing that. I liked to be at the back. I didn't like anyone right behind me. That would worry me hearing that blade so close. I remember once they somehow got me in the centre. I think I was following my brother, and there was another one behind me. "You carry on," I said, "I'm a-goin' to the back." And I did. But we never got any accidents.

'Sometimes you'd get a bit of competition between some of these old boys. The Lord, my word he'd slip into it, and he'd shout, "Come on," and the others would have to keep up with him. We had to mow at least an acre a day.

'Of course, they stopped scything when the binders come in, but before them we had the sailer reaper. That would push out the sheaves, but we didn't often tie them because, if the barley was ripe, as that would be, the straw was too brittle. So we'd rake the sheaves together so that the ears of one were just overlapping the other. Then when it come to picking them up, you could put the fork under the first one, double it over and pick the two up in one. You could do that lovely if you got the people to rake that in the right way. But when the reapers-and-binders started coming out that was a different thing. They bound up the sheaves for you, so then we had to set them up in shocks.

'Mr Lilley liked to have a stetch[1] of about eleven feet . . . well, eleven feet two inches to be exact. So if you mowed down the field the way it was ploughed, you got more stubble in the furrows. When you cut across the field - not going the way of the plough - you could sweep it out nicely. That was the idea of it.

'A six-acre field - and the six of us would have that done in a day. I have heard men say that they've done an acre and a half a day. Well, maybe they have if they've started pretty early, but if you start at six in the morning and cut an acre a day each, you can't grumble at that.

'They'd often sow clover seed in, when drilled the barley, for winter feed. So you had to scythe that down with the barley, and that didn't cut so well. That made the work harder. But the clover would come up again and be

---

1 Suffolk dialect: the ploughed land between furrows. See page 61

43

harvested in the spring.'

For mowing barley the scythe was fitted with a hoop. This enabled the corn to fall neatly, the more easily to be gathered into sheaves, if it was not to be left lying loose as was the custom with barley. The hoop could be an iron fitment or a withy cut from the hedgerow. For mowing wheat the scythe was fitted with a slightly more elaborate attachment, like a shortened rake with long tines, known as a cradle. Its purpose was also to enable the corn to fall into bundles so that it was easier to tie up.

It was in this first year of George's man's harvest (1911) that Mr Lilley had a small reaper, known locally as a sailer or ribber, to cut the wheat. The machine had four or five wooden sails each with a row of wooden teeth or pegs. As the sails went round they swept the corn, as it was cut, on to a platform, and then dropped off sufficient to tie a sheaf.

'You wouldn't sweep the cut corn off with every sail, because there wouldn't be enough. It all depended on your crop. If it was a stout crop, then you could put the corn off on every other sail. You could set the sails so that one sail would miss it and the next would sweep the corn off to make a sheaf. But, as I say, it all depended on your crop, because you didn't want to make your sheaves too silly big, because in wet weather that took longer to dry through.

'With barley we usually had to mow with a scythe, but if the sailer was used, then you'd often let it put the barley off with every sail, especially if you'd got clover in with the barley. The clover had got to lie there to take all the sap out of it. Then when it had dried off it would shake out, otherwise if you gathered that up and stacked it the stack got too hot and discoloured your barley.

'We were still tying the wheat up into sheaves by hand, but for barley that was different. You didn't bind that up. When you cut it by scythe you had one long swathe, and when you wanted to cart it, you had to go along with a rake and pull so much one way and so much the other, just to make way for the cart. Then, as I say, we used the two-tine fork to lap the ear ends of one lot over the other. That would then be ready to put in the stack with the ears of the barley on the inside to protect them from the weather.

'Of course when the reaper-and-binder come in that cut the

corn and bound it, and then the barley had to be put into shocks¹ like the wheat. But sometimes if the weather was right, if that were a hot summer, we didn't trouble to shock the barley. That would be loaded straight on to the cart and go to be stacked, or even go straight to the thresher.'

During the harvest the men worked from six in the morning until nine at night, and Mr Lilley never stinted them for beer.

'If you were working near the farmhouse, he'd bring out a twelve-pint can of his own brew. Well, with just four or five of us, we didn't need it, because we'd mostly got our own beer we'd brewed at home.

'Mother always made harvest cakes at this time. They were square currant cakes about the size of your hand, and very nice they were too.² I would leave mine for beavers,³ as we called it. That would be about five o'clock for half-an-hour. Then we'd go on again till dusk.

'There was something else mother used to make for harvest time too, with bread dough and onions. The onions would be partly cooked and then put into the dough and sealed in. By the time the dough was baked the onions had finished cooking. We called them dannocks.⁴ Sometimes I'd have them for dinner or breakfast. They were very tasty.'

The end of reaping always found the harvest field full of people, and of children especially, because as the last of the corn fell there was the chance of a rabbit for the pot.

'Even as a lad I would get down to the harvest field. I loved to run after a rabbit, and I'd catch one, too. I was pretty nimble then. I'd have a nice stick and sometimes you could walk round and see the rabbits run up and down the ringes.⁵ If you looked at the crop you could see it a-movin'. You'd think to yourself,

---

1 Suffolk dialect: sheaves set up endwise to dry.

'The mowing of barley, if barley do stand
is cheapest and best for to rid out of hand,
Some mow it and rake it, and set it in cocks,
Some mow it and bind it, and set it in shocks.'

- Tusser.

2 In my own family erroneously called 'short-cakes'. - HS.

3 Suffolk dialect: the afternoon equivalent of elevenses and sometimes called fowerses - fourses.

4 Moor does not give dannock at all, but Claxton defines it as 'A kind of cake made of bread, dough, sugar, fat and raisins', which seems nearer to George's harvest cake than to his own description of a dannock.

5 Suffolk dialect: a row, 'the channel in which seed is sown'. (O.E, *hringe*.)

45

"Right, I'll get him". Then, as the reaper come down, he'd be running ahead of the machine, and then you could just catch him with the stick. Sometimes if you saw one go under a sheaf you could pop down on the sheaf and pick it out, and then ring its neck. I've caught many like that, and I've run and caught them too. Sometimes they'd be running like mad among the sheaves and one would bounce into a sheaf and get underneath it. That's when you could catch him all right. Then you'd hulk[1] it, take it home, and the next day someone would skin it and that would be cooked for your supper the next night. That would make a nice feed. I used to like a stewed rabbit, or a rabbit pie.

'Well, that's how we had to live, and I often think back to those days. Today you've got your big food manufacturers, and that's all manufactured grub people are getting today. I don't think you can beat the plain way we used to live.

'There were hares in the harvest field too, but we didn't try to catch them. We had to leave them for the shooters, when they came round later. Except perhaps for the farmer's son there were no guns in the harvest field. Mr Lilley wouldn't allow that. We just had our sticks, but I always got a few rabbits.'

Customs of ancient and religious origin have always been associated with the harvest, but modern machinery, which has displaced the man-power and animal-power upon which agriculture depended for centuries, has driven out the old and ritually significant ceremonies. Although the Lord of the Harvest still existed when George began his working life, the duties of the Lord, after the harvest, had already been abandoned. At the harvest feast or horkey, held when the last load of corn was taken to the farmstead, the Lord led the 'hallooing largess', and also solicited largess from his master's guests.

George remembers the word 'horkey' used to describe these occasions, but says that Mr Lilley never held a harvest supper of any kind. 'I've heard people talk about them, and a right merry time they seemed to have, but I never went to one, and I don't think the farmers round here held them.'

In fact, there is little doubt that the horkey died out at the beginning of the present century. Thomas Tusser, the sixteenth

---

1   Suffolk dialect: to disembowel a rabbit or hare.

century Suffolk farmer, agricultural writer and versifier, refers to it thus:

> 'In harvest-time, harvest-folk, servants and all,
> Should make, all together, good cheer in the hall;
> And fill out the black bowle of blythe to their song,
> And let them be merry all harvest-time long.'

Although the horkey had vanished, the ritual observed before it was still practised. 'When we took the last load of corn home, we'd draw up beneath a tree, and pull down a green bough to put on top of the load. Oh yes, that was a proper do that was. That was quite a game among the farms to finish the harvest first. Sometimes, on the next farm, they'd know how close you were, and so they'd stick up two or three green boughs, so we should think they had finished. We used to do it too, just for a bit of fun, but it was the last load that really carried the green bough. I don't know why that was done, but it had always been the custom.'

Even that ceremony has disappeared with the coming of the voracious combine harvester, but in earlier times the green bough would have been decorated with streamers and either a girl would sit on top of the load, or else a dolly of corn would be fashioned from the last sheaf and placed there. But whether it was a girl, a corn dolly or, as in George's time, a green bough, it represented Demeter, the Greek goddess of corn-growing and agriculture. It was, in short, a pagan fertility custom.

Although there was friendly competition to be the first to complete the harvest, an exchange of yarns in the pub at the weekend kept all the farmworkers appraised of their neighbours' progress.

'Well, that's all we'd got to talk about in those days. We'd challenge each other like: "I think we can beat you this year. We shall finish 'haps Tuesday night, maybe earlier". But, of course, we all knew how long that was going to take. It depended on the season, and no two seasons were alike. If you could start harvesting in fine weather, and that held, then you could go on and finish harvesting, and if you'd got a sort of medium crop, then it would take about a month to clear, to cut and cart and rake the fields and then gather up the rakings. If you started in the last week of July, you could get done by the middle of August. But if you had a wet time, well that flung you. It didn't matter much about carting wheat a little bit on the damp side, but barley - they were more particular about that. But a nice dew on it in the morning didn't hurt, and you could gather it all right.

'Although there was no kind of celebration once we'd got the harvest in, we did have a day out if we possibly could. Perhaps we'd go up to Colchester (11 miles away) for the day, and my brothers might go to Clacton by horse and coach. They'd walk to Hadleigh and pick it up there about six o'clock in the morning. They'd get as far as Manningtree and have a break to rest the horses, and a drink and a piece of something at the pub. Then off they'd go to Clacton. And what time they got home at night, don't ask me. That could have been midnight, or even the next morning. But I never went myself.

'Oh, we were soon back at work. After harvest you had something else to face, and that weren't very nice either - muck-spreading.'

7
From Stacking to Stockman

Harvesting was not complete until the corn was safely stacked in the yard ready for threshing. The finished stack, properly thatched, was a fine structure in which the men took pride. A yard full of well-built stacks was an advertisement for the farm and a testimony to the skill of its workers. The thatching, however, was not done by any of the farm labourers. It was a task for the local thatcher. Most villages had their own resident thatcher, and Polstead and Boxford were no exception. Thatching was mostly done with wheat straw. Reeds, which give a better and longer-lasting cover, were reserved for the cottages and houses of those that could afford them.

The average stack was about nine yards long by five yards wide. 'You might want to keep a certain field to itself in the stack. Then, if you'd got any gumption about you, you'd know how many loads would come off that field, and you'd build the bottom of the stack according to what you wanted, but that was usually about nine by five. That needed a good foundation of thick straw. You had to have it at least a yard thick if you wanted to keep your bottom layers. Later in my life when I used to go threshing, at some farms, when you picked up the bottom sheaf, you'd ofttimes see the ground behind you. Well, that corn would have to be thrown out. That was no good at all. But if you put a good straw bottom down, then all the corn you took up was good. That is if you'd made the stack properly.

'We would have three or four men making a stack. There'd be the unloader. He'd pass the sheaves to a chap on the stack. He'd pass them to another, and that one would pass them to the stacker. You always had what we called the arse-ends of the sheaves outwards. That's how we used to stack them - the grain inwards and the arse-ends out, and you slant them down, so the centre of the stack was a bit higher. That helps to shelter the grain,

49

so that when the roof came on top, the water will come off the thatch and keep the foot of the stack dry. Ofttimes that would stay in the stack quite a long while before that was threshed. A lot of barley would be left until the winter, unless the corn merchants were calling out for it.

'If you could really get at it - say four men in the field a-loading and four men at the stack - you could build a nice nine-by-five stack in a day.'

The corn in and stacked - then came the muck-spreading. This was the manure of the stockyard with its mixture of straw that had been used for bedding. It was the only kind of fertilizer used on Mr Lilley's farm. Although some of the muck was carted straight from the yard and heaped out on to the fields ready for spreading, much of it had been carted earlier in the year and made into muck hills, where it composted before being used after the harvest. Thomas Tusser has his own words for these heaps of muck:

'Or ever you ride with thy servantes compound
to carry thy muck-hills on thy barley ground:
One aker wel compast is worth akers three
at harvest thy barne shall declare it to thee.'

The cleaning out of the stockyard and the carting of muck was usually done sometime in June, after the haymaking.

'We carted the muck on to the field by horse and tumbril, tipped it out and spread it to form a dungle.[1] That had to be properly made, because that would be five or six feet high, and packed down so that didn't overheat. It would be left until the muck spreading in the autumn, before the winter ploughing. Then we would cart muck from the dungle into the field, putting it down in heaps - eight yards from one heap to another, seven heaps to the load, and ten or eleven loads to the acre.

'It was just the same if we were carting straight out from the stockyards, but it was better if it had been left in the dungle for a few months. That's a lot better than the artificial fertilizers today. That help to keep the land open. I don't think there is anything to beat nice farmyard manure for the land.

'Well, once that was put out in heaps we had to spread it ready to be ploughed in. We did that with a four-tined fork. Today, I know, they've got muck spreaders and loaders, and all the hard

---

1 Not given by Moor, Forby or Claxton, but George insists that 'dungle' was the word used locally. It's presumably a corrupt form of dung-hill.

50

work is taken out of farming. But you really felt you were doing something in those days.

'The muck was ploughed in ready for drilling wheat and barley, but oats - well, you didn't often manure much for oats, because that would be your last crop before a fallow - a long summerland[1] - though sometimes we'd plough and muck a piece of it and put in mangolds and swedes. After the summerland that would be sown down to wheat and barley. The next year that would be beans or peas with some clover, or sometimes the clover would be sown down with the barley the previous year. Then that would come in for wheat again[2] Mr Lilley farmed on a four-year rotation. That's different today. With artificial fertilizers it's wheat after wheat, barley after barley. And I don't reckon that do the land any good.[3] That take too much out and that don't put much back. Of course I know they've got different qualities of corn today, but to my way of thinking it's not such good quality as it was when I was young. There's more of it. They go in for quantity not quality. What's more the straw was used in my day. That weren't burnt. The farmers had to leave it for thatching and so on, but today that go into the combine, that's broken up ready to plough into the ground if they like to take the trouble. But they don't do that. They just put a match to it, and I think that's stupid.'

George was not called upon to help with the threshing in these early years of his working life. That was to come later. But with muck-spreading and threshing done, he was occupied with various jobs in the barns, the most important of which was probably dressing the corn.

The corn-dressing machine was a kind of wooden cabinet with a hopper at the top and a handle at the side, which was turned to rotate four wooden blades. There was what George calls 'a slip' in the hopper, and this was used to regulate the amount of corn that went through on to the sieves beneath. Turning the wooden blades created a wind inside the cabinet and joggled the sieves. The wind carried away the chaff and the corn seed fell on to the sieves and ultimately out of a shute at the side of the machine. Sometimes the corn was dressed to provide seed for

---

1 Fallow land; land left clean and uncropped throughout the summer.
2 George is describing the system of crop rotation known as the Norfolk four-course system, in which crops are rotated in four groups. It was devised by Charles (Turnip) Townshend and Coke of Holkham.
3 While this is true of some farmers in the neighbourhood, there are, to be fair, others who still adhere to a modified system of crop rotation.

Mr Lilley. But if there was a good sample, especially of barley, then he would sell it.

From day work George graduated to stockman. This was to be preferred in those days when farm workers only got paid for the time they worked, and bad weather meant no work and no pay. There was always work for the stockman to do - feeding the cattle and sheep, mucking them out and generally caring for them.

'I had to be up at least at half-past five - well, more likely five o'clock, because we had to be at work by six. A wash in cold water, and perhaps a small bit of something before going off. But as for breakfast, I'd got to feed all the cattle before I could have that.

'During the winter Mr Lilley would buy his steers in at Michaelmas, and then fatten them up. I could have about twenty or more to feed. Then there was a yard full of pigs. I'd got to feed the lot before breakfast - that's in two-and-a-half hours to half-past eight. From then on, I had to prepare for the night's feed and the next morning's feed for the bullocks. So when I started in the morning at six, I'd already got the feed I'd prepared the day before. I used to grind up enough mangolds to last through. Of course, they had chaff and cake, but my boss didn't like mixing the cake with the other food.

'Out in the yard there was a big pen, rather like a cattle market, and that had one manger in it. I'd have about eight bullocks round that, and about another dozen or more under cover. When I started feeding them I'd give them about half what they should have. Then I'd go and feed the pigs, and then come back and give the bullocks the rest of their feed. Before I started I had to sweep the mangers out nice and clean, so that the bullocks could eat their cake separate.

'The pigs were fed on meal, but you couldn't prepare that the night before. It had to be done in the morning, and after they'd been fed I'd mix it up again ready for the afternoon. The pigs were kept in a brick-walled yard on the other side of the farm. That more or less joined the house.

'Of course in the right hot weather, I couldn't even mix up the cattle feed in advance, because that might go off - a wee bit on what we'd call the sour side. So in the hot weather I'd mix it up just before I fed them.

'He had a little flock of sheep as well, about sixty, I'd say. There weren't as many sheep in these parts as there used to be in the old days. Mr Daking had around three hundred, and Mr Partridge had some as well. They'd shear the sheep for the wool as well as sell the lambs. But Mr Lilley bought his sheep - mostly Southdowns - at the lamb sales at Ipswich in July, just to fatten them up. He'd run them on his stubbles after harvest, carry on until winter, and then there'd always be a few acres of swedes. We'd go out and top and tail them, and leave them in heaps. Then in the winter he'd have a machine out in the field with a big hopper on it. It was my job to fill that up with swedes and grind them up for the sheep.

'If the weather was too wet, we had to take the sheep off and run them on the meadow. He never lambed any - just fattened up the lot and sold them off. They'd all be gone by March. Then the land would be ploughed up and that would come in for barley.

'But swedes are beautiful things to eat. I love swedes, much better than potatoes. If my mother had cooked any and we hadn't eaten them all in one day - well, they'd come in lovely for breakfast. Just warm them up, or fry slices of them. That's no wonder in the army we old Suffolk boys used to be called "swede-knawers".

'After I'd fed all the cattle in the morning, I'd have my breakfast. In the hot weather I'd get outside and sit on the grass to eat it, but not in the winter, I can tell you. Sometimes I'd have a slice of pork or . . . well, you couldn't always have meat in those days, and so then that would be bread and cheese and an onion. My dinner was practically the same, because I couldn't get home for that. So I took it all to work in a bag. You could buy calico at that time of day, and mother would cut it out and make food bags of it.

'We never cut up bread and butter into sandwiches like they do today. Mother would cut off a big piece of bread, then cut a hole in the top and put the butter in. Then she'd put the piece back on top. That's how we used to do it. Then you had your cheese or, if you were lucky enough, a piece of meat, or there might be an egg. I had a tin to put them in. I always took a bottle of drink. That was mostly cold tea. If you drank that before dinner, then you had to make do with a bottle of cold water for the rest of the day. Sometimes if you'd got a few coppers in your pocket and you fancied a pint of beer . . . well, you'd just walk to the pub. That took about a quarter-of-an-hour to get there. But often a pint would help you for the rest of the day.

'After breakfast there'd be the night's feed and the next morning's feed to get ready. Then I might have to get some hay in, and sometimes there'd be foddering to do - that's getting the straw into the yards. Foddering the bullocks would mean there'd have to be a couple of men with a horse and tumbril loaded with straw. Then when they tipped that out I had to spread it around.

'As a rule, Fridays would be my day for cleaning out the pigs. I had to clean all the sties out, and then put the fresh straw in, so they had a nice clean weekend. Then I'd do it again on Tuesdays. My boss was very particular over his pigs. He liked to see them kept clean, and that was a good thing too. I liked it, that I did.

'I would start feeding in the afternoons about three o'clock, and then I'd got two-and-a-half hours. Mr Lilley didn't like me to feed them all at once. "Give 'em time," he used to say. Then you could see if the bullocks wanted an extra bushel or two. And the same with the pigs. I would give them just so much and let them lick the troughs out nice and clean. They'd tell you more or less if they wanted any more. Then you could go and equalize[1] a bucketful out. He didn't like to see them overfed, so that they left food in the troughs. "Do you give 'em what they want," he said, "but don't overdo it".

'He didn't go in for breeding pigs. He just bought them, fattened them up, and sold them. Sometimes there'd be a hundred or more. He used to have the Gloucester Spot. We called them plum puddings. They were brown and white. Then he had a black pig - the Essex, I think it was. There was a man near the Chantry at Ipswich and sometimes he'd come along and buy the lot.

'Then I'd have to drive them to Hadleigh station.' (Hadleigh is about 3 1/2 miles north-east from the farm and was then on the main A1071 road to Ipswich; now it is by-passed, and the station closed.) 'You couldn't do that today. I've been up at four o'clock in the morning summer time, and I'd be down at Hadleigh station with them at six.

'Someone would help me over Hadleigh Heath, or into the straight road where the chapel is. Then it was left to me, and I had a lot of running about, I can tell you. If there was a gate open anywhere, they'd be through that like a shot. Then I had to get

---

1 I haven't been able to find any record of the word used in this context except by George. - HS.

them out, and do the best I could. After a time they sort of tired themselves out, and then they'd go down the road all right. It depended how much trouble they were as to how long it took. Sometimes it was three hours. I've even been out at three o'clock in the morning when it was light. Then I'd get to Hadleigh before the heat of the day got up.

'Sometimes Mr Lilley would make his mind up all of a sudden and take them down in a horse and wagon. That were an open wagon with a pig-net over it. That was mostly winter time when he decided to do this. Otherwise, in the summer, he'd tell me to drive them. Then they went from Hadleigh to Ipswich by train.

'You seldom saw much on the road at that time of the morning. But there was always one chap I met. He used to come from Hadleigh through to Sudbury in a horse and cart with the East Anglian paper. Makin was his name. And in the winter time, when the snow was on the ground - I know we got more snow then than what we get today - that was the only track you'd see on the road. Winter and summer he was always there.

'We used to drive the fat bullocks down to Hadleigh too. They were kept in the yards until they were fattened up and ready to go, from March onwards. Then after we'd got rid of the bullocks, I had to clean out the yards.

'Now that don't do any good to muck them out in the winter time, because, with the bullocks there, that all gather heat, you see, and if you clean them out, you're letting the heat out, and that put your bullocks back.

'It's surprising the yard never got really mucky, not even in wet weather. But with the straw and the muck and everything on top of the concrete, that really got hard. Then in the summer time, after the yards had been cleaned out, they lay open to dry ready for the next winter.

'The cattle were free to go into the shed at night if they wanted to, but some would always lie out in the open.

'If the boss bought some extra bullocks, then he didn't like to mix them. So we'd part them off from the rest in the yard with posts and rails - good wooden rails. I had to help Mr Lilley do that, and I liked that job. We dug holes for the posts, and we didn't concrete them like they do today. We just rammed the earth back. He bought good wood for the job, and we nailed the crossbars to the posts.

The bullocks were all kept at Sprotts Farm, which Mr Lilley had hired, but the cows were kept at the Brewery Farm. They'd come in at night, except during the summer. Of course he wanted me to learn to milk the cows as well as look after the stock, but I wasn't having that. I mean as it was, as stockman, I had to go twice on Sunday - morning and afternoon - to feed the cattle. But I had to learn. I soon packed it up. I told him "I can't do it. I get cramp in my fingers," I said. And I just didn't do it. I wouldn't learn. I didn't think that was a job for me any old how. I didn't want to be a milkman.'

Although George turned away from this additional skill - largely from a feeling of being put upon - he was, like his father and brother Jack, a regular breadwinner, and there was always the need to earn a few extra coppers for such necessities as boots and clothing. It was important to have something that would keep out the cold east and north-east winds. Corduroy trousers were most effective for this purpose.

'You needed them if you were stuck out in the fields in a wind, I can tell you.'

The top garment was usually a jacket or a waistcoat, or even a pullover knitted by wife or mother, and beneath that was the all-important shirt. That had to be warm and keep out the wind. Some were made of calico. We had something called the Oxford shirt. Mother made them, and they were like the others, only coloured with stripes. I don't know why it was called Oxford. Then you needed leather gloves for some of the rough work, like hedging, and we had to buy them. You could get them in the village, or at Hadleigh or Sudbury.'

One of the ways of contributing to all this necessary expenditure was collecting rats' tails.

'We got a penny a tail from the schoolmaster.' (The old penny; six old pennies are equivalent to 2 1/2 new pence.) 'I don't know who it was who ran the scheme, but Mr Bromham was made responsible for collecting the tails and paying for them. I was working at the Sprott's farm at the time. We had meal bins there, and the corn stacks were built in a big hollow area that had been cut out of the hill. Well, the rats used to play havoc in those stacks, and they would burrow into the bank where it was sandy. There were rabbits there as well. I don't know why the rabbits and rats lived together, but they did somehow.

'The rats would travel along the building where the meal

bins were, and I used to catch them in traps and snares. Every time I went in I'd see rats. So I thought I'd have a little scheme of my own. I got a piece of wire and made a snare and stuck it up in one corner where the rats always ran. I'd made it just wide enough for their heads to catch it. Then when they ran through it that pulled tight. The weight of the rat did that. So they'd let go their hold on the wall, and then they just hung there. Oh yes, I've caught many like that. The boss used to laugh at me. He thought that was quite clever.

'Well, I remember once taking about eighteen tails to the schoolmaster. He paid me and told me to destroy the tails. But I took them back to the farm, and kept them till I'd got some new ones. But I didn't get quite enough for my liking the next time. So I put in some of the old tails. He guessed what I'd done. He said, "I think you've got one or two in there that you brought me last time." I didn't deny it. I just laughed. Anyhow, he paid me.

'I used to take him sparrows' eggs as well. We were paid a farthing an egg.' (A quarter of an old penny.) 'That was to keep the population down, because there was an enormous lot of sparrows about then. They'd build in the thatched roofs and do a lot of damage, and whenever we fed the hens in the farmyard with corn, there'd be more sparrows than hens to pick it up. So they were a proper nuisance. Any road that were another way of earning an extra penny or two.

'Much later than this - after the first war when battery torches were about - some farmers and their sons would go round the yards shining these bright torches. Two or three of them would hold up a big net and then brush the roof where the sparrows were dazzled by the light, and catch them that way.

'I was careful not to go for rabbits in the stack yards because there were cats about there, but I'd often catch a rabbit out in the fields, either with a stick or a catapult. If that were a sunny day, an old rabbit would often sit on the sunny side of a big clump of grass. Well, if you just cock your eye and see him there and then strike down quick enough with a stick, you'll get him.

'Also in the winter you could see their runs, and if you put a snare down you'd most likely catch one. Then I was quite handy with a catapult. If I saw a rabbit on a bank, then I'd like to be about three or four yards away, and I'd be able to get him in the head quite easy. I've caught several like that with a catapult, when I was working for Mr Lilley. He never said anything. He didn't mind you

57

getting a rabbit or two, but I don't think he would have liked it if you'd made a habit of it in working hours. I watched out for them during my dinner hour. I'd walk round very quiet, and perhaps spot one on the bank somewhere. I could make eightpence of that, sometimes ninepence if that was a nice young rabbit. That was how I used to get my pocket money.

'My weekly wage went to my mother, so anything I got after that helped to buy my boots and clothes. I bought my boots from Mr Gardner in the village. He didn't make them, but I know what he called them: *Time will Tell* - that was the name of the boot, and they were pretty good. I think they cost about seven-and-sixpence or ten shillings.' (37½p or 50p.) 'That was before the first war.

'Of course there were a fair number of hares and pheasants, but we daren't touch those. I suppose there might have been one or two who had them, fellows who'd got a gun. I never had a gun, and I never went poaching either. I shouldn't say there was a lot of poaching round here. There could have been the occasional one or two, but you never heard much about it. We knew the pheasants weren't for us, and that was that. We were a fairly law-abiding lot.'

8
Ploughing

The horseman - the head man - was responsible for ploughing. He drew the first furrow. Its straightness was his signature, recognizable by every other ploughman in the neighbourhood.

While George was stockman he was not required to learn the ploughman's skills, but one Michaelmas morning, a few months before he was twenty-one, he took out a pair of horses and a single-furrow plough for the first time.

It was 1914 and Britain was in the first weeks of war. The affairs of Serbia, the assassination of the archduke and his duchess in the streets of Sarajevo by a Serbian student, and even the shipment of British armies across the Channel to France, still seemed distant events to those in the barleyfields of Suffolk. George remembers how he first heard about the declaration of war.

'When I went to work on the Monday morning, my boss said, "The war has started." I said, "What war?" He said, "Didn't you hear about it?" He'd got it in his paper, the *East Anglian*. "Well," he say, "they've declared war." "Oh," I said, "we shall have to go up then." "They won't want you," he said. "That'll soon be over." "Well," I said, "may do, we shall see." But we were really under that impression - that it wouldn't last many months. That didn't seem real somehow, not that it could go on. Not natural, if you know what I mean.'

So George remembers that at this time there was a sense of unease throughout the countryside - a not a fully understood knowledge that there was a war somewhere over there, that wasn't part of the life he knew and yet was going to affect or change it in some way impossible to know. Its most notable effect for his family, and for others like it in the village, was an almost immediate increase in prices. Already it seemed that war might mean hardship.

But it was a clear fine morning when Mr Lilley confronted him with: 'Do you come down to the stable. There's a pair of horses there. I want you to go to the plough.'

'I said, "Whoa now, I don't know nothing about that."

'"Well, you'll have to learn," he said. I said, "Right." And I did. I learned to plough, and that weren't much trouble really.

'The reason he took me off stock work was because there was another young lad - the head horseman's son - who'd just left school, and he wanted the job. So he took over from me when I went on to horse work.'

From his childhood George had enjoyed being among horses. He appeared to have an instinctive understanding of them, and they responded to him. The one essential for a good working relationship with a horse, he maintains, is kindness.

Mr Lilley never kept pure bred Suffolks - those beautiful and enormously powerful horses with deep and wide chests and slender strong legs. So George began to plough with two crossbreds.

'One was named Scott, the other Matchet. They were two bay horses, one a bit darker than the other, and the darker one had got white stockings.'

The single-furrow plough which he used was the famous Ransome YL - a plough that was introduced in 1843 and was still being used a hundred years later. This was an iron plough with two wheels, built so that the larger wheel would run in the furrow and the smaller land wheel on the surface. It was made by Ransomes, Sims and Jefferies of Ipswich. Robert Ransome (1753-1830) was the founder of the firm of agricultural engineers which still bears his name. He invented the process of chilling cast iron, and so produced the first self-sharpening cast-iron share in 1803.

'The head horseman just showed me how to pull the wheel up or drop it, according to how deep you wanted the furrow. Then he showed me how to alter the hake of the plough - that's the front part of it. If you wanted to take a full furrow all the way, you just haked it off to the right a bit, and that pulled it to the ground.'

The hake, sometimes called the bridle, was fixed at the very front end of the beam - the main wooden or iron curved bar running the whole length of the plough to which all other parts were attached - and it could be adjusted both horizontally and vertically to determine the depth and width of the furrow to be ploughed. A chain attached it to the pommeltree which, with the whippletrees that were connected between the plough and the horses, helped to distribute the load evenly.

'The old ploughmen before me had the Bentall plough.' (It was made by Bentall of Maldon, Essex.) 'That had a wooden beam and just one wheel, and they used to enjoy that. Well, some of the old horsemen, when they got the Ransome iron plough with the two wheels, they'd take the furrow out and still use just the one. They liked to be as straight as ever they could, and they could manage better with one wheel. But you'd got to balance the plough then. But if you'd got two wheels, then you could just set them according to the depth you wanted, and that was easier. At least that was for me.'

George quickly learned to draw a straight furrow, although he never regarded himself as being among the top-rank ploughmen.

'I liked to go as straight as I could, 'tis true. I wanted to be as good as anybody else, but I wasn't, and that's the truth. Sometimes I would make a bit of a mistake. I might get a little bit of a wind in it, and 'haps another time the next furrow would be dead straight. But some of the old boys - oh dear, they wouldn't be an inch out. They used to have ploughing matches. I never went in for those. But some of them would be less than three-quarters of an inch out. That's pretty good going. But I never classified myself as a tip-top man.'

Arthur Young described the ploughmen of Suffolk as 'remarkable for straight furrows; and also for drawing them by the eye to any object, usually a stick whitened by peeling, either for water cuts, or for laying out broad ridges, called here *stitches*; and a favourite amusement is ploughing such furrows, as candidates for a hat, or a pair of breeches, given by alehouse-keepers, or subscribed among themselves, as a prize for the straightest furrow.'

In Suffolk the fields were, as Young says, ploughed in stetches. The word seems to have originated in the county. A stetch is the ploughed land between two furrows; in effect, stetches are strips of ploughed land with a deep furrow on each side to drain away the water. They varied in width according to the nature of the soil. So narrow stetches of six or eight feet were used in the heavier land to enable the water to get away, but obviously the wider the stetch the less land was wasted, and the wider stetches also provided larger and better seed beds. George ploughed in stetches of eleven feet two inches, which seems to have been fairly common in this part of Suffolk.

'The head horseman would draw the first furrow, though I've done it many a time myself. First you'd put up a stick, perhaps a peeled hazel stick, at each end of the centre of a stetch. Then you'd set your plough into those two sticks, and that's how you could go straight. One man could plough up to an acre a day,[1] and by the end of the day he would have walked ten or eleven miles.'

This first shallow furrow and the second furrow done on the return was known as 'opening up the furrow'. The next two furrows, cut deeper so that the slices fell into the first furrow, were known as 'laying the top'.

'On my third day of learning I shut up my first furrow. The chap who was showing me said, "You're doing all right, and I'm going to learn you now to shut one up." So he haked the plough a wee bit and showed me how to take one furrow off - taking up the brew we used to call it.'

The brew or mowle furrow was the last in the stetch. It completed the stetch, and it was essential that all the brews should lie the same way, otherwise the stetches would be of different widths, and then the drill wouldn't fit them when it came to sowing the corn.

'The drills in those days would be six-foot drills. So they used to straddle a stetch in a bout - that's once up and once down. That's what we called a bout. Only when you came back you wouldn't need the outside coulter on, so we used to block that off so no corn went down. I remember that was the Smythe drill.[2]

'Of course much later they had steerage drills. They didn't go up and down. They used to go across the stetches.

'Although the fields round these parts were full of flints, we didn't have much trouble with them. Today they plough with tractors and go down, some of them, a foot, but at that time of day, when we were using horses, if you went down six or seven inches deep that was the very most. You ploughed a lot more shallow those days. My boss liked me to plough no more than about four inches deep - for wheat especially. But if you were ploughing a

---

1 In many parts of Suffolk a horse ploughman was expected to do three-quarters of an acre a day.

2 James Smythe of Peasenhall in Suffolk first began making peg drills in 1830, but the six-foot drills followed later. His most popular model was the Nonpareil, which was produced in 1860.

field that was going to be a long fallow for next summer - summerland we used to call it - then you could go deeper, perhaps six or seven inches. That's a good depth, you know, for a horse. But for drilling, we'd plough about four inches deep.

'The deeper ploughing today could be a wee bit better, because when you turn the soil up deeper there are minerals down there. And another thing, when you go deep the soil is more pliable, and that don't become stagnant when there's a lot of rain. The water's got a chance to go through.

'Of course we had to do what they call sub-soiling - that's to get the drainage better. You could always see in the winter, if the water couldn't get away, the fields that needed sub-soiling. There'd have to be two of you to do that, one following the other. The first man would be ploughing about six inches deep. The second man would follow, only he'd take the breast off his plough, so he was just ploughing with the share and trying to get deeper. That was quite hard work, hard work for the poor old horses, too.

'Mind you, much later on, come the 'thirties, they'd got different machinery. I remember a thing called a gyro-tiller. That was a big machine, and that used to twizzle and stir the ground round and round, and that would go down eighteen inches or a couple of feet easily, and over a width of nine or ten feet too.'

Harrowing the soil after ploughing was a particularly essential part of cultivation on the heavier soil of West Suffolk, and although the disc harrow had been patented more than half a century earlier they were not in use on Mr Lilley's farm. George used the rhomboidal harrow.

It was a frame set at an angle with four or five bars on it, and there'd be three or four tines driven through each bar. Because they were set at an angle, it meant the back tine would break the soil the front one missed.

'First we'd go over the land with a heavy harrow, and then there'd be a medium-weight harrow, and once we'd drilled the soil we went over it again with a light harrow - that was just to cover up the seed.

'Usually one man would be breaking down the ground before drilling. Then on the day we drilled that used to be my job to do some more harrowing in front of the drill. Then afterwards I'd have to hook on the light harrows and dress it up. We called the last harrowing that covered up the seed dressing up.

'I didn't always get it done, because I mean they liked to do

63

ten acres a day drilling - that is, if the ground weren't too heavy for the horses. When it began to get a bit wet then that was a little stiffer work for them. My boss didn't like to see you overwork the horses. He liked a certain amount done, but you weren't to drive the horses to get done within a certain time.

'Mostly the horseman would have a bit of food at eleven o'clock - elevenses - and then he'd carry on until three o'clock, and that's when he stopped for dinner. Then he'd take his horses back. But oft-time when we were drilling I'd carry on till four o'clock to get the seed covered up. Then I'd go back to help the other man to get the hay in for the night. After that, I'd push off.'

Here George is describing what was the ploughman's usual day - beginning at six-thirty in the morning and ending at two-thirty or three o'clock in the afternoon, when the horses were returned to the stables to be fed. The horseman, however, would have arrived at the farm about four-thirty in the morning to feed and groom the horses before taking them out for their day's work in the fields.

'It was hard work. But then there was nothing else for it. It seemed right, and you didn't hear much grumbling. There was the work to do, and that was that. For me it was from six in the morning to half-past five at night. There were no half-days. We didn't get a half-day till 1926. You worked six days a week. And if you were a stockman, which is what I was till I was eighteen, you had to work on Sundays too. So did the horseman. Cattle and horses have to be looked after, Sundays or no. I can't see youngsters doing it today. But I didn't mind. It wouldn't have made any difference if I had. That was the way of it at that time of day.'

9
Chapel

An almost fatalistic acceptance of the conditions of his life and of the natural order, rather than an active belief in God, characterized George's early religious awareness. There were certain things that were not questioned, merely because they had always been part of the daily pattern of life. Chapel had been one of those unquestioned features during his childhood, and so it remained now that he had grown up. Since the family had moved down the hill into Boxford, however, he no longer had the three-mile trek to Hadleigh Heath, but went instead to the Congregational Chapel in the village. (It is now the United Reformed Church.)

This is a solid, square red-brick box built in 1823. It stands near the top of a gently rising street, curved like a long S, and filled with terraced houses. Tudor facades are jostled by Georgian and Victorian frontages. Many of these later faces are false. The stud and plaster of Tudor buildings lies behind them, and beyond those and beyond the chapel itself, the arable fields slope up towards Groton and Edwardstone.

The habit instilled by his devout mother did not die easily, but he no longer accompanied her to chapel now that he was a young man. He went instead with some of his pals, although the whole of the Everett family attended the services.

'Boxford Chapel was crammed in those days. You got all the Edwardstone and Groton people too, especially on Sunday nights. I went morning and night. Mornings were at eleven and evenings from six-thirty to eight or after. Well, there was nowhere else to go, nothing else to do. That's not like that today.

'It was a nice service. They had long sermons in those days - about three-quarters of an hour. Sometimes the regular minister would chop over with one from somewhere else; then the service would usually be a bit shorter. And we used to sing those rousing Sankey and Moody hymns.'

From his boyhood, chapel funerals had acquired an especial importance for him, although he found it difficult to explain why.

'If there was a funeral on, nine times out of ten it would be on a Sunday. They used to bury on a Sunday then. I would always go, and that made me think about things - the end of people I'd known. I don't say I liked going, but I would think to myself, "Well, I've seen the last of Mr or Mrs So-and-So", and that was so final that it made me think that perhaps we ought to try to lead a good life. There was my mother, of course, always ready to do a good turn, and I think I took after her a bit. So I seldom missed a funeral. To me they seemed more important than christenings. I never went to those.'

George had already come to live in Boxford when he made his last and sad visit to the chapel at Hadleigh Heath. It was 1913, and a young girl who had lived next door to them at Bower House Tye died.

'Her name was Ethel Holmes. She would have been about thirteen. Poor girl used to have epileptic fits, and when she died, Mr Holmes - he'd already lost his wife - wanted four brothers to take her to the chapel. So there were my brothers Bill, Jack and Arthur, and me. I was the youngest. We had to carry her for a mile on our shoulders.

'I remember my father, who was nearly always a bearer for Mr Mann, the carpenter at Hadleigh Heath who used to do the undertaking, I remember him saying to me, "When you go past the corner of the chapel to the graveyard, watch out for the little ditch. That's not very deep, no more than a foot, but if you slip you'll catch the weight." And so I did, but anyhow I was fairly strong, and I got through that all right. But that's when I began to think about things - that perhaps we weren't picked out for a long life, and perhaps there was some meaning in that youngster's death and we should all try to understand. I haven't been into that chapel from that day to this.'

For his mother, however, belief and faith were incontrovertible and nothing kept her away from the chapel. Although by now George was attending the Boxford Chapel with some of his fellow farm-workers, there was no one outside his family with whom he had a close relationship. There were no special mates. It was the example of his hard-working father and the gentleness of his mother that remained the predominating influences. Not until after her death in the nineteen-thirties did George stop attending the chapel services.

But much of the habit of attendance was, as he says, because there was nothing else to do, and there were no means, other than walking, of escaping from the village community, where the demands of cultivation determined their way of life.

Thus it was on foot that George made his way six-and-a-half miles to Sudbury fair to see the first moving pictures. 'That would be 1913 or 1914, and I can't remember now what it was I saw, but everybody was talking about it, and so I wanted to see it. That was in a tent on the gaswork's meadow, and after I'd looked at the flickering pictures I walked the six-and-a-half miles back again. But then, wherever you wanted to go, you had to walk. We didn't have bicycles. There wasn't enough money to buy things like that. But you thought nothing of it. If you wanted to go, you walked.'

So the Chapel, without modern distractions, exercised its influences primarily through habit. This did not mean, however, that old superstitions and customs, which over countless generations had provided the alternative religion in the country-side, had much significance for George. He was too practical to heed them or even to remember many of them. The exception was certain weather signs, which experience had taught him were invariably accurate as a means of forecasting.

'Now with animals, especially bullocks, if that was going to rain they would start to play about. And pigs - have you heard that saying that the pigs can see the wind? I don't know if that's right. After all, that's invisible. But they can scent it, I reckon, because if you see pigs a-picking up the straw and playing about with it and running with it, that's a sure sign of rain. I think that was a pretty good sign too. Sometimes they'd seem to go proper mad, and that would always rain afterwards.

'Then in the summer time the poor old horses would get tormented by flies. Whenever that happened we used to say, "We're going to have a heavy storm, there's thunder about." And nine times out of ten that was true. As soon as that started thundering the flies to go, and the horses were all right again. I would try to help the poor things by cutting a piece of elder[1] from the hedgerow. If you tied that to the

---

1   In East Anglia elder was also regarded as a protection against witchcraft.

bridle, or pushed it through, so that rested along the neck, that would keep the horses' heads all right. That was the smell of the elder, I think, that kept the flies away. Sometimes though I'd get a thick bag and split it and put it over their backs, just to stop the flies biting.

'There's another thing - a horse will never pluck at elder. If you've got two horses on the plough, side by side, and you put a bit of hazelnut or maple between them, one of them will turn his head and pull it out, or have a bite at it. But if you put a bit of elder between them, they'll never touch it, and that do seem to keep away the flies. They used to say, too, that it was unlucky to burn green elder.

'If that were very cold when the blackthorn flowered, we would call that a blackthorn winter. We had another saying about the weather. That's a well-known one.

"Ash before the oak,
Sure to be a soak;
Oak before the ash,
Only be a splash."

But I don't know if that was always true. But "a mackerel sky forebodes rain", there might have been more in that. Another was, "When it rains with the wind in the east, that do rain for twentyfour hours at least". There was another little rhyme that went,

"Near burr,[1] far rain;
Far burr, near rain".

And they did say that if the gulls weren't following the plough, but were all over the field, it was a sign of rain. But if the new moon was lying on her back that was a sign of fine weather. But we didn't take a great deal of notice of the old superstitions, although that were a common belief that if you brought hawthorn blossom indoors it would bring you bad luck. And some didn't like lilac indoors either.

'We had certain customs about planting. You had to put beans and peas in at the growing of the moon. As the new moon came in you planted your beans and peas.'

This does not accord with practice in all parts of Suffolk. The moon undoubtedly had a great significance for countrymen because it was so closely linked with the weather, but there is a difference of opinion about the sowing of peas and beans. An old

---

1 The halo round the moon, signifying fine weather when it is near the moon.

rhyme has it:

> 'Sow peasen and beans in the wane of the moon,
> Who soweth them sooner, he soweth too soon,
> That they with the planet may rest and arise
> And flourish with bearing most plentifull wise.'

George's verdict on that was: 'That may be so in some parts, but in this part of Suffolk we always said you had to sow your peas and beans at the growing of the moon, and never at the wasting of the moon, else they'd waste too. Still, I wouldn't always go by that. I used to like to cock my eye to the weather. I reckon that was a better guide.

'Then potatoes - you never put them in until Good Friday. A lot of old boys used to say that Good Friday was the time to start gardening, and not before. It didn't matter if that were an early Good Friday or a late one, they wouldn't do anything until that day. There was only one thing they would sow earlier. Put in shallots on the shortest day and you reap them on the longest day - that's what they said, but I don't think that very often happened like that. I mean the shortest day is more or less winter, and you couldn't always do what you wanted because the ground would be frozen hard. That really make more sense to pay attention to the weather.'

This observation is typical of George's practical nature. In the past the countryman lived with the weather. It determined his way of life and he learned how to use it to his advantage, and stoically accepted those times when it appeared to work against him. Something of this heritage had been acquired by George. Perhaps it was the fact that, when the weather was bad and you couldn't work on the land, you didn't get paid, that made George especially aware of it. In any event, he can go back to the early years of this century and remember the day and the date of great winds and storms or snowfalls. It is, however, May 1924 that is etched in his memory as the year of the worst storm in his experience.

'I was working at Polstead, and all the morning it was a-thundering. That laid out Colchester way. Then, at three o'clock in the afternoon, that broke - a terrible storm - thunder, lightning, and torrents of rain. I weren't surprised. That morning I'd noticed the pigs a-messing around. Well, going home we had to wade through water above the knee. When we came to Tills Farm, where Sam Fletcher lived, they had been spraying the road with tar and chippings. He'd got the front door and the back door of his house open, and the water was rushing through in a great flood and carrying barrels of tar with it. Blast, that was a sight.

'Butchers Lane was flooded, about a foot-and-a-half deep, but that just didn't get into number six. A little girl was sitting on top of the wall that go round Peyton House opposite, and she was laughing at people having to wade through the water. She was the child of Mr and Mrs Hoagen, who had just moved into Peyton House, and that night, by the light of the moon, they were struggling to move their pigs indoors, because there was so much water about. Oh, that come down off the fields, and there were faggots and branches of trees floating everywhere.

'We kept the water out in 1924, but we couldn't stop it in 1947. That had been a sharp winter, and the thaw started on 12th March. On the 13th water was rushing down the lane from all directions. The River Box overflowed and flooded The White Hart pub and the post office.'

Among his weather memories George is adamant about one thing: 'Nearly every Christmas when I was a lad, there was snow and ice about. Winters, like so much else, seem nothing like they used to be.'

10
Beer and Wine

George's employer, Mr Lilley, was a successful farmer who supplemented his income by brewing, and the home farm was called Brewery Farm. Lilley attended to the brewing process himself, and afterwards delivered the beer throughout the neighbourhood - more, it seems, to private customers than to public houses.

'He would go as far as Stratford St Mary and Dedham.' (About seven and eight miles from Boxford.) 'His customers would buy four-and-a-halfers or niners.' (The reference is to gallons.) 'Mind you, he never used his own barley. He made sure he'd sell that, and then he'd buy his malt from Mr Kemball in Boxford or a Mr Mason at Kersey.'

As the industrial revolution mostly by-passed Suffolk, the importance of Boxford as one of the wool towns declined, but other industries developed, including the making of gloves and parchment, and the brewing of beer. At one time there were twenty-two maltings in the village, and even White's *Suffolk* of 1844 records: 'Boxford has several well-stocked shops, good inns and a number of malt kilns.'

By the time George was a young man, however, they were all gone except the malting owned by Mr Kemball, which stood at the entrance to Butchers Lane, the narrow lane in which George has lived most of his life. Another malting - at Peyton House - on the opposite side of the lane, was knocked down in 1922, but it had already ceased working in his youth. Only brick panels in the boundary wall now mark the places where barley was shot from carts in the lane.

Mr Kemball's maltings were in the middle of the village, and George himself remembers delivering barley there from the farm.

'That was a busy village in those days, with horses and wagons piled with grain. A lot of fellows would tie them up in the yard of The White Hart, or take the horses out, and put them in

71

the stables there, so they could have a bit of food in the pub in peace.

The trade was much more towards Hadleigh than Sudbury, than it is today. You see, you'd got the maltings at Hadleigh - Wilson's maltings. He was a corn merchant too. He used to buy a wonderful lot of barley and wheat and oats. From all around they would go to him. And there was Mr Gayford, another corn merchant there, too. Oh yes, the road was very busy sometimes with horses and wagons.

'Mr Lilley would brew three sacks of malt each week, and in the summer, when he had a bigger trade, he had three big brews a fortnight.

'After Mr Kemball or Mr Mason had delivered the malt, me and my brother Jack had to grind it ready for brewing. Mr Lilley had a mill that was worked by hand. It was a bit like a mangle with two rollers. There was a sort of hood where you put the malt in, with a little slip to regulate how quick you wanted it to come down on to the rollers. You could also regulate how fine you wanted to grind the barley.

'That would take me and my brother about two hours to get through three sacks. I'd be one side and my brother the other, turning the handle. There was a little spout to the thing, so that the crushed, malted barley ran off into a sack. Mr Kemball's malt was just nice. That was easier to grind. But sometimes we got some from Mr Mason that was on the tougher side. You had to get the rollers close, and then that was harder for us to turn.'

Mr Lilley brewed his beer in large vats, and George's brother Jack spent a great deal of his time washing out and scouring the casks. The job of racking the beer Mr Lilley always reserved for himself, but the activity of brewer as well as farmer, meant there was always plenty of beer for his workers at harvest time. He was, it appears, generous with the allocation of his home brew.

'But he never drank his own beer. In fact, I don't think he drank much at all, and he very seldom smoked. He told me once that he never smoked. Then one day when he came out to give me some work to do, he'd got a cigar in his mouth. I said, "I thought you told me you didn't smoke?" He laughed. "Ah, that's one I had given me," he said.'

Mr Lilley's generosity with his farm brew, however, did not relieve the Everetts of the necessity of brewing their own beer. This was a domestic tradition which had existed for countless

72

generations in the cottage homes of Suffolk. In the Everett household it was mostly the task of George's father, but sometimes of George himself. They always brewed for the harvest, but 'there wasn't beer in the house all the year round. Chance times perhaps my elder brothers and my father managed to get the money to buy a couple of bushels of malt. Then we'd make another little brew, but that would be the lot until the next harvest.'

A bushel of malt and a pound of hops would make eighteen to twenty gallons of beer. The brewing was done in July and began about two o'clock in the morning.

'We had what we called the mash tub. One of us would shoot the malt into it, and another would stir it. The copper was lit to boil up water, and we put in one gallon of hot water and two gallons of cold. Then we stirred up the malt with a masher.'

This is a long-handled wooden implement, like a very large wooden spade, the blade of which is a frame of open bars. This is used thoroughly to stir the malt.

'There was a tap on the mash tub, and at about five or six in the morning we'd drain off the liquid into another tub, put a cloth over the top, with the masher to hold it in place, and leave it for about four hours. Meanwhile we boiled the copper up again for the second mash. More water was added to the remaining malt and that was stirred and mashed again. The second wort was boiled up with the rest of the hops. Of course, it was never as strong as the first brew.

'After the first brew had been standing for about four hours that was put in the copper and boiled. Then you added about three-quarters of the hops, and you boiled the whole lot for about another four hours. Then that was left to cool and a pint of yeast was added. You had to let that stand until the next evening, and then you skimmed off the yeast and ladled the beer into casks. Of course they'd been well scrubbed and aired already. Usually we would mix the second brew with the first, and then you had a really lovely beer.

'It wasn't as bitter as modern bitter, but that was a lovely deep amber colour. Mind you, the colour depended on the malt, but Mr Kemball always had a beautiful malt, and when we got it from him, as we mostly did, the beer came out a beautiful deep amber.

'But I'll tell you what I used to like to do. After the first mash - that was before the hops were added - I liked to drain off a

73

mugful and then let it stand to cool. The sweet-wort, we called it, and that was real nice - very sweet that was.'

The home-made beer would be left in cask for at least a week before drinking. Helped by the generous rations of beer given by Mr Lilley to his workers in the harvest field, the Everett's home brew would certainly last through harvest and usually beyond. It would have been capable of keeping for at least a year, but never survived that long.

The boiler was used not only to make beer, but to do the weekly wash, to heat up water for a bath, and to make wine. The Everetts were not big wine makers, but they made it from time to time to supplement the beer and as a special treat for Christmas. Rhubarb, bullace, elderberry, red currant, plums, damsons, parsnips and mangolds were all used to make wine. The family would never start to drink it until at least a month after it had been made, but it could have been kept for many months.

'My favourite,' said George, 'was mangold wine. If you kept that for about nine months it was like drinking whisky - beautiful.

'We sliced up the mangolds and boiled them, I think for about a couple of hours, and then it had to be strained off into a big container, and when it was cool enough you put the yeast in to work it. You had to let it ferment a bit. Then you put it into two-gallon stone bottles. That would take some time to ferment, and you'd often have to take the cork out, or that would burst. If you were lucky you might get a four-and-a-half gallon vinegar cask from the grocers. That had a little vent hole on top, so you could put a peg in it. Then when you heard it a-sizzling you could ease back the peg until it quietened down. Then you knew it was ready for drinking.

'We made parsnip wine the same way. That's a heady wine too - soon put you on your back, that would.

'I remember once I was ploughing - that would be with a tractor about 1929 or 1930 - on a field at Bower House Tye. A Mrs Leeks lived just over the hedge. She called out to me and said, "Would you like a glass of wine, George?" I said I would that. So I had this glass of wine, but that were really a little beer glass. "Oh, that's beautiful," I told her. "Well, that's cherry wine," she say. So I went on ploughing, and a bit later she called me again and gave me another glass. "How do you like that one?" she asked. I told her that was very nice too, and she said that was wheat wine. That was just like whisky to look at. Well, just before I had my dinner, she called up again and said, "Would you like another tot of wine, George?" I told her I thought I'd better not have any more. But she brought me this glass and said that was potato wine. "That's all right," I said, and I knew it was, because that had got hold of me lovely.

'Well, I daren't get off that tractor, I can tell you. I just had to go on up and down, up and down. I'm surprised the furrows were as straight as they were. Anyway, that wore off after a bit, but oh dear, that was powerful stuff. She made all sorts of wine - beet, mangold, wheat, potato, cherry, plum, apple and dandelion. And that's a very nice wine. But, as I say, my favourite was mangold wine.

'When my father was dying, he asked for a little drop of mangold wine, and when the doctor came - Dr Truman - he said that wouldn't do him any harm, but it wouldn't do him any good either. We knew he was dying then. But when the doctor came down from father's room, he asked if he could try some of the wine. So he did. "Cor," he say, "that's just like whisky." And that was, too.

'Some people round here also made wine from wheat, and from the Polstead cherries. And that was really beautiful. There's nothing like a good glass of home-made wine.'

Except perhaps a glass of the home-brewed beer. But then beer was the farm-worker's drink, and it was recognized as an essential part of his daily food.

11
Off to War

During the early months of the war not much news filtered through to the village. Some men had been in the Territorials, and a few others joined up immediately on the outbreak of war. Occasionally a family lost a son or a husband, and the village shared in the grief and the mourning.

'I remember early on one fellow coming back from France. He'd been in the trenches, and he'd still got blood on his great-coat. I knew it wouldn't be long before I'd have to go.'

So as the months lengthened, the war at last began to have its impact upon the village; the men started to leave; and the Army came to look for horses.

The work of the land was more urgent than ever, but so was the demand for transport, and that meant the four-legged kind. Some farmers hid their horses when the Army came looking for them, either because the animals were too valuable on the farm, or because their owners could not bear to part with them.

George remembers a couple of officers visiting Mr Lilley's farm, looking at the horses, and making an offer for one of his favourites - the bay with the white stockings, Matchet. George took the animal, and another from a neighbouring farm, to Ipswich, where the Army were making use of a local sale yard.

'There was a sergeant-major there, and I told him where we came from. We exchanged some papers, and I handed the horses over. He said to me, "Well, are you going to stay with them?" "No," I said, "I shan't do that - not today, I won't. I'll leave it till after Christmas." '

George returned to the farm, but already he knew that in a few months he would be leaving his Suffolk home for the first time in his life. Until then, the fifteen-mile journey to Ipswich was the furthest he had been.

Early in the new year of 1915 there was news of Zeppelin raids on the coast. It was said that Great Yarmouth and Cromer, in Norfolk, had been bombed, and in April a Zeppelin dropped bombs on the Suffolk coastal towns of Lowestoft and Southwold.

Full reports of the raid were given in the newspapers, but rumours were as freely available as fact, and they penetrated as far inland as Boxford. It was even said that the Germans were going to attempt an invasion from the sea.

George decided he would wait no longer, and in May 1915 he returned to Ipswich to join up.

'It was Whit Tuesday, and I joined the RASC. They sent me home for a week and told me to come back the next Monday. So I did, and I found they had put me in the Suffolk Regiment.'

He had led a healthy open-air life and was undoubtedly strong, but on the day he joined the Army, George, at five feet nine, was slight of build and weighed no more than nine stones. He was a handsome young man, with a long oval face, well-set eyes, and a strong nose. He also boasted a crisp, slanting moustache.

George was immediately packed off by train with all the other recruits to the barracks at Bury St Edmunds to be kitted out.

'There was one old soldier there who showed us how to roll our puttees. You had to start both from the inside, but some boys had a lot of trouble with them. You either got them too tight or else too loose round the ankles. Anyway, after about a week most of us could do them all right.'

The following day George left for Felixstowe, where he did his infantry training. He was billeted in a house in Queen's Road.

'We slept on straw palliasses laid on three boards on low trestles. We had to fill our own straw matresses. And we were issued with rough brown blankets.'

At night in the billet, during the day on the field behind the railway station, where the young recruits did their arms drill, or by the sea front, where the bayonet fighting was done, George still heard the familiar Suffolk voices around him. They helped to assuage the empty feeling of absence from the people and surroundings he had known all his life. He was reluctant to acknowledge homesickness, because in his practical-minded way he knew that what he was doing had to be done, and he might as well get on with it and make the best of it. Sometimes he thought of the possibility of being killed, but considering it more for the effect it would have upon his parents and his home than as something to be feared for himself.

The raucous shouting of orders, sergeants who treated rookies as though they were imbeciles, the marching up and down, the drilling with the Lee Enfield Mark 3, the proximity of the other men, sweating and swearing, the ribaldry of this new khaki life, were all an incongruous contrast with the low moaning of cattle before being fed, the grunting and rooting of pigs, and the soft plod of the horse drawing the plough, and yet George found he was adjusting rapidly, without thinking too much about what was happening.

'I never thought about the reason for the war, or anything like that. We weren't thinking of politics at that time. It was the war, and that was that, and I had my training to do. You were supposed to be a fully-trained soldier in three months. Well, I didn't find it all that difficult.

The training in bayonet fighting we did near the Pier Pavilion on the sea front, unless it was wet, and then we went into the pavilion. We had to charge with our bayonets into huge bags. Of course you didn't get any leave until your training was done, and I was a bit unlucky, because there was another young fellow with the same name as me in the same company. He always seemed to be the lucky one. But eventually I came home on draft leave, and I remember going up to the farm along of my father and giving him a bit of a hand in the harvest field. That all seemed very strange after the bayonet practice.

'Then when I got back I found I'd been picked for the draft for Egypt. But when I went in front of the doctor again, he wouldn't pass me fit, although he had passed me before I'd gone home on leave. He said my ticker was affected a little bit, and I'd have to give up smoking. So I did. Well, you couldn't do much smoking, because your money wouldn't allow it. I got seven bob a week, and when I joined up I asked that half of it should be sent home to my mother. So all I had was three-and-six a week (17 1/2p) and you didn't always get that. Sometimes something was knocked off for barrack damage. We were billeted in houses, but if any damage was done we all had to pay.

'But sometimes I managed to go to the Felixstowe Playhouse. That was a cinema, but there'd always be a turn of some kind or another as well as a picture. That helped to pass the time, but at the weekends the usual thing was a sing-song and a dance in the pub. That didn't matter which pub you went into there was always someone there with an accordion.

The beer was better then, and I think it was a bit darker too - tuppence a pint for mild, and there was a very dark and strong beer at thre'pence a pint.

'Altogether I spent a year at Felixstowe, and then joined the London Regiment for service in France. I shall always remember the day I left because it was the day Lord Kitchener was drowned. The King came down to Felixstowe to inspect the troops. He got off the train at Felixstowe station and went across to the Orwell Hotel, and that was where he received the message about Kitchener's death.

'There were a hundred of us from the Suffolk Regiment that went to London that day. I shall never forget it, because when we got off the train at Liverpool Street station, we had to march to Waterloo, and we even got jeered at as we went through the streets of London. People shouted at us that we were conscripts. I suppose that was because they had taken our numerals and our cap badges away from us as we were going to join another regiment. We went on to Winchester, and that's where we joined up with the 24th London Regiment. That was June 1916.

'We stayed at Winchester for a week, and then sailed for France. We went overnight from Southampton to Le Havre. That was a calm night, and our lot went below decks. I remember thinking to myself, "Well, this is it, boy," and wondering where we were going and what it would be like.

'When we got to Le Havre we spent a week under canvas. Then we set off up the line to somewhere near Loos. It was the first of July - the day the battle of the Somme began.'

12
Into Action

On the 4th July 1916, as an infantryman in the 1st 24th London Regiment, George first went into action in the trenches. This was at Bully-Grenay, about three miles south-west of Loos. The great battle of Loos had been fought the previous year, and in September 1915, there had been an Anglo-French advance on a front from Le Bassee to Lens.

'There was a thunderstorm the day we went in. Rain poured out of the sky. There was mud everywhere, and you had to slop through eighteen inches of water in the trenches. I was soaked through.

'From the trenches you could see Loos in the distance, bits of jagged ruin sticking up. The landscape ahead of us was fairly barren - great tracks of churned up earth and craters where the shells had fallen. It was pretty bleak I can tell you. I reckon there was between a hundred and five hundred yards of no-man's land between us and the Germans. You could see their ridges of sandbags - drab and grey, like the whole of the landscape. That looked desolate and miserable, that that did, especially with the rain a-coming down, and entanglements of barbed wire scrawled all over the place.

'On that very first day an officer told us all never to put our heads over the top. A few minutes later he did it himself, looking through his glasses across the wasteland. He was shot through the forehead and fell back into the mud, dead. That was the first time I'd seen a man killed in the war. Before then I hadn't really thought about it. You didn't, you know.'

George spent three weeks in the front-line trenches, armed with the Lee Enfield rifle. It had a magazine capable of firing fifteen rounds in thirty seconds. He soon became used to the screech and shattering sound of shells from both sides in a series of barrages every day. At night, with bayonet fixed to his rifle, George went out on patrol, led by the platoon sergeant. The night would be lit with the flash of gunfire, and the air filled with the sound of shells tearing up the sky, as the platoon moved cautiously through the gaps cut in the barbed wire.

'Our job was to try to capture Germans and bring them back for interrogation. We went out in an A formation, and if the leading man saw anything, we would draw back into a straight line. If the German patrol kept coming, we used to fall back to form a V.

'You had to be wary. Both our sappers and theirs used to tunnel out under no-man's land, and then there were the shell holes. You had to be careful that you didn't drop into a nest of Jerries.

'Sometimes we would exchange fire with a Jerry patrol, but none of the patrols I went out on ever brought back any prisoners. Still, I was lucky not to cop it there. We were moving about pretty near Jerry, and most of the time we were being shelled. Or we'd hear their rifles and machine guns, and blast, the sky would be all flashes from the guns.

'Living in the trenches wasn't much fun either. As I remember them now, they seemed always to be wet and smelly. Yet they somehow seemed safe, especially when you got a bit of sleep on the wire mattresses. But you couldn't keep the lice away. Everyone had his own way of trying to deal with them. I used Harrison's pomade. I'd put it round the top of my shirts, under the arms, and round the neck. That did stop them. But you were so filthy with mud and muck that you couldn't keep them away. Whenever we had a fine day I would try to wash out my shirt and freshen up. But that wouldn't last for long.

'I can't really remember the fellows I shared the trench with now. That was so short a time. But I do remember a feeling of comradeship, of all being in it together - the wet, the mud, the filth, the stink. And sometimes one of them would cop it, another get wounded and moved out of the line. They used to think that was lucky - to get to Blighty as they called it.

'But I think I was lucky, lucky to survive, and not even get wounded. When I first went in, I thought of what my father used to say: "We're here today, boy, and gone tomorrow". But I can't honestly say I felt afraid. I used to think to myself: "Well, that wouldn't do to be too nervous. I knew we were out there to do a job, and there wasn't any alternative. So I just got on with it. I don't think I was ever very nervous. 'Tis true, that was not a nice feeling, and all sorts of things would go through your mind when I thought about home. I used to wonder what ever would happen at home if I got popped off. Still, I thought to myself: "What is to be will be. If you get hit, you get hit." But I was pretty lucky.

'I thought about home a lot. It was about harvesting time, and I thought what it was like just a year ago, and now here I was in the mud and the trenches, and things going off all round me. And I would wonder how they were getting on, and whether the wheat and the barley were going to be got in all right. I wrote letters home whenever I could, and when it was impossible, then I'd send a field card. But after the war, there were two long tins full of letters I'd sent to my mother. When she died I put the letters from one of them in the coffin beside her.'

When George was pulled out of the Loos sector, there began the gradual trek to the Somme. First Vimy Ridge, then Arras, but in neither place did he see any action and, after a while, he moved down to Millencourt and Albert, Fricourt and Mametz, but by the time he reached the fighting lines on the Somme his role had changed.

He recalls the long march down to Millencourt, because it was the time of harvest. Many of the villages behind the fighting zones were comparatively untouched. He remembers going through village streets of whitewashed houses, and beyond them, fields of corn still being harvested despite the deadlocked but devastating fighting that was going on not so very many miles away. The woods had trees full of leaf, not like those he'd seen stripped to splintered stumps by shells.

Sometimes the roads were liquid with mud, sometimes dry with caked mud and dust, often lined with trees, and mostly busy with lorries and trucks, despatch riders on motor cycles, limbers carrying supplies, and columns of soldiers weighed down by their packs and rifles.

In the distance could be heard the boom and reverberation of heavy artillery, and at night the sky was spattered with flashes of light and the probing crossed beams of searchlights, and the red dots of anti-aircraft fire. They trudged, singing and whistling their way to the Somme or, as they tired, marched in an uneasy silence, each man locked into his own thoughts. George wondered what it would be like. There had been stories of enormous losses of life,[1] and stories, too, of German prisoners in hundreds, glad to be out

1 On the first day alone nearly 20,000 allied soldiers died.

of the fighting. Yet George's main feeling was one of resignation because of the inevitability of what was to come.

It was during this march to the Somme that an orderly sergeant asked for volunteers for the transport section, and preferably he wanted men with experience of looking after and handling horses. That was something George did know about. He volunteered and, after he had explained about his work with horses on the arable fields of Suffolk, he was accepted at once. This meant no more fighting in front-line trenches, but the equally dangerous task of carrying supplies at night up to the front line under a regular barrage of shellfire.

During the day the horses had to be watered and fed, looked after and kept clean, and still invariably within the range of enemy shells. But this immediately gave George another interest, something different from the weary acceptance of trench warfare. Moreover it was an interest rooted in the rural traditions of his own countryside. He found in it a reassurance, an affirmation of values that he had come to understand.

It was now that he met Kitty and Ruby, two golden-coloured mares. These light bays were to be his close companions for the next two years - on the Somme, at Ypres, and on the Somme again.

13
'Something was about to happen'

Within a day or two a close relationship had been forged between man and animal, as George came to know the different temperaments of his two horses. For his part he was attentive and gentle, kind and understanding, and the horses responded with a comparable devotion.

'They adapted wonderfully. They seemed to take everything for granted, including the shellfire. They were two very sensitive animals, but they never got alarmed. They seemed to understand that there was nothing I could do about the noise and the flashes, and the jets of earth that were thrown up when a shell burst nearby. Somehow they got used to it. A few soothing words, and they trudged on. And they were jolly good at night. We had no light, remember, when we were taking supplies to the front. You had to feel your way through the dark, and there was nothing for it but to leave it to the horses. They wouldn't make a false step. If there was a shell hole they'd see it. You couldn't, but they could, and they'd pull round it. And it didn't matter if all hell was let loose and the sky flashing all round, they knew when to go on. We had to take up whatever was wanted - rations, sandbags, trenching tools, small-arms ammunition.

'The two horses were harnessed side by side, and I used to ride Kitty. She didn't like being made a fuss of so much as Ruby. I always had a slab of chocolate with me, and if I got a piece out while we were going along the road, Ruby always knew. If I held a piece up, she'd turn her head round and take it, without interrupting her stride. She's even taken chocolate from my own lips.

'I know once when we were back at rest somewhere - I can't remember exactly where it was - the brigadier came round, and he pulled out a bag of sweets. He was offering them to his colonel and his transport officer. But they weren't standing more than a couple of yards away from my own horses. I thought to myself, "If

84

they see you with those sweets, they'll want one". And they did. The brigadier stood with his back to them, and before he knew what was happening Ruby put her nose on his shoulder. I told him I thought she wanted one of his sweets. He gave me a couple, and they each took them out of my hand. They were lovely old horses.'

Feeding the animals with hay and oats, and watering them, not to mention trying to groom them, was never very easy when they spent their whole lives in the open, in all weathers, usually tethered to a rope slung between a couple of limbers. These daily chores were accompanied by the booming reverberation of the railway gun and the more sporadic outbursts of heavy artillery. Even during the day they were invariably within range of enemy shells.

By this time George was lying up on Mammetz heights ready for the great push of September 15th 1916. On his way there from Millencourt he had to go through the shell-shattered town of Albert.

'I remember the red-brick tower of the cathedral with its arches and columns. Great holes had been blasted in the body of the church. That was crumbling into rubble. But the tower, although it had got bits knocked out of it, still stood and there, right at the top, and leaning over at an angle of about ninety degrees, right over the street, was the figure of the Virgin Mary. You could see its gilt in the sunlight. Why that didn't fall I shall never know. It looked as though there was nothing keeping it up.

'The French used to say that when that fell the war would end, but I think that was a bit of wishful thinking, because it looked as though it would fall at any minute.'

The roads around Albert at that time, pitted and broken by shells, were full of lorries, wagons, horses, ambulances, field hospitals and field kitchens; and the landscape sloped away pock-marked and scabbed by craters and dugouts and trenches.

'Although it was a depressing sight, there was a lot of activity going on, and you felt something was about to happen - something more, I mean, than the bombardments that went on most of the time.

'It was somewhere near Albert - it might have been at Méaulte - that I saw what seemed hundreds of German prisoners. I remember there were still trees there - tall and in leaf, and buildings standing. And there were these huge batches of prisoners.

'All of us had been surprised, since we'd been on the Somme, at the numbers of captured Jerries. After the barrage of shelling, you wouldn't think they could have survived. But they did, and hundreds of them were collared. And many of them looked pretty cheerful, I can tell you. They looked glad to be out of it.

'I remember standing on one side of the village street, with the trees behind me, watching the prisoners go by. I stood alongside my pal, Ginger King. All of a sudden one of the prisoners shouted out, "Hello Ginger, how are you, mate?"

'Ginger said, "I'm all right. What are you doing here?" I thought that was a damn funny thing to say, and the prisoner grinned, and said, "I'm happy all right now".

'The prisoner-of-war camp was not far from our village. So at night we went up to it, and there was this prisoner walking round by the wire fence. So we stood and had a good conflab, and then he said, "Ginger, you think the Germans can bombard, but by God we've had it up there. Thank God I'm out of it now". It seems that he had worked with Ginger in London. He couldn't get over the coincidence of meeting like this, and was as pleased as Punch to see Ginger again.

'What was so strange really was that it somehow seemed natural to meet in this way as friends. In other circumstances Ginger might have killed him, but here they were chatting away like good old mates. Things like this made the war seem unreal, and yet there it was blasting away all the time, and your mates getting killed. It made you wonder if it was all worth it. Sometimes I would think, "I don't know whatever we're born for, to go through all this - to kill one another. That don't make sense to me. I don't think we're sent on this earth to kill one another." Whatever it's done for , I don't know. Greed, I shouldn't wonder. Yet I tried not to think too much about it, because there was nothing I could do, and there was no sense getting all in a lather about something you couldn't help.

'I remember our going through Fricourt on our way to Mammetz. That was a sight. I don't think there was a brick or stone left in that village. There was rubble everywhere, and not a sign of life, except for our own stuff on the roads. The bricks and stones from the battered villages were used to make up roads, but it was no sooner done than there were shell holes all over the place again.

'And beyond was the wood, if you could call it a wood. The land here was sort of rolling upwards, and there wasn't a leaf to be seen on the trees. There was scarcely a tree. They were just like a lot of huge splinters sticking up in the ground. Everything else was grey and bare and a mass of craters and wire entanglements. The rims of the shell holes reminded me of grey waves, rolling down towards you.

'We'd had some hot days, and that somehow made it look even more unreal than when it was raining and there was mud and filth everywhere.

'We had been surprised at the numbers of our men getting killed, but when you saw this you could understand how it had happened.

'I wondered again how long my luck would last.'

14
To the Somme and back

George arrived on the Somme in good time for the third great offensive planned for the 15th September 1916. A number of attacks were carried out on various sectors of the front earlier in the month to prepare for the major offensive to come.

'The road from Fricourt, along the valley of the Willow Stream, we used to call Death's Valley. That used to get shelled such a wonderful lot. All the way to Guillemont, at the end, beyond Trones Wood, you were under continuous fire. That road was open and bare except for a few twisted and broken stumps of trees. At Trones Wood, I remember, was a crucifix corner. I can see that crucifix now and, with all the shelling, that hardly got touched.'

Guillemont fell to the British on the 3rd September, the day when an unsuccessful attack was mounted at noon on High Wood, more than two miles to the north-west. Two months earlier men of the 7th Dragoon Guards, the 20th Deccan Horse, the 1st South Staffords and the 2nd Queen's had crossed the ripening cornlands and fought their way into the wood which, in spite of an earlier bombardment, was still full of green leaf. As dusk fell they were stopped by German snipers, rifle and machine-gun fire. Now the wood, still in enemy hands, had been shell-stripped of every leaf with branches splintered from the trunks. These stood in jagged columns with still some tangle of growth beneath. On the 8th September the 2nd Welch and the 1st Gloucesters again tried to fight their way into the trees during the early evening, but again had to withdraw.

During these attacks in early September George was taking supplies up to the lines near Bazentin le Petit, a little to the left of High Wood. There were days of driving rain, and the roads and tracks were a sea of mud. Supplies were taken up at night by horse and limber.

'There'd perhaps be a couple or three for the rations. Then there'd be a limber for small-arms ammunition and hand-bombs.

And then perhaps you'd have to take a water cart up as well, and there'd be a limber for sandbags or anything else they wanted. Usually four limbers used to go up. Oh, that wasn't all sunshine, I can tell you, but we knew we'd got to do it, and you had to use your own initiative if you wanted to get back alive.

The corners were the worst. That's where Jerry put down most of his shells. Either they could hear you, or they knew within a little time when you were going up with the rations. So you had to time it. If they were shelling a certain distance away, you'd count the salvos. I used to get in as close as I could and then, in the pause in the shelling, I'd push one limber through. It wouldn't do any good trying to get them all through at once. You'd be sure to lose someone. So you had to ease up and watch for the next salvo. Sometimes they'd come about every three minutes. You had to judge where the shells would fall, and then take advantage of the gap. Well, that's how I used to work it anyhow, and I was pretty lucky getting through. I knew the old quartermaster wouldn't go up the line if I didn't go up too. He used to say that I was the luckiest one. None of the chaps who went up with me ever got hit, either going up or coming back.'

It was during these days of forcing his horses and limbers through the mud with supplies for the big push to come that George had an experience that brought back, with a vivid nostalgia, memories of his life in Suffolk.

On his section there was one water point where he had to go to load his water cart. 'One day there was an artillery bloke there with his horse. "Do you know," I said to him, "that little horse you've got there, I think I knew her in 1914." He stared at me. "Go on," he said. "Yes, I believe I did," I told him. I looked at her, and I knew her all right. She was a bay and she'd got four white stockings. "I don't know what you call her now," I said, "but I know what we called her when she was broken in for work." Then I called her. "Matchet," I called. She pricked up her ears at once. She was the same horse, that she was - the horse that I took to the Army at Ipswich. When you work with a horse and get to know her, that's like a friend. You always know her.'

Matchet was one of the two crossbred horses that George used when he first learned to plough. That day at the water point on the Somme was the last time he saw her. He never discovered what happened to her after that, or if she survived the war.

On the day of the big offensive tanks were used in warfare

for the first time. They had been preparing less than thirty-five miles from George's Suffolk birthplace. At Thetford, on the Norfolk-Suffolk border, they began assembling in June 1916. Kitchener had regarded them as of limited military value and described them as 'a pretty mechanical toy', but in the forest and on the heathland and arable fields near Thetford they exercised before being shipped to France to enter battle on the Somme. General Robertson, the Chief of the Imperial General Staff, wrote to Haig: 'I hope the tanks prove successful. It is rather a desperate innovation.'

Men in transport, constantly moving from reserve to forward positions and back were well-known as carriers of gossip, rumour and information. They invariably knew when something was afoot, and George was sure another big offensive was imminent. Artillery had been bombarding the German lines incessantly. The 12th September had been a warm day, but the 13th brought more showers before a fine, sunny and warm day on the 14th. The big push was launched at twenty minutes past six in the morning of the 15th.

'That morning, I was standing on the road leading from Crucifix Corner up to High Wood. The noise was deafening. Our guns were firing all the time at Jerry. Some of our aeroplanes were in the sky too. While I was there I saw the first tanks go by. They were going into action at High Wood. Later I heard we'd lost a lot of men that day before the wood was taken.'

A.H.Farrar-Hockley in *The Somme* (Batsford 1964) records that of 24 tanks that were the first to go into action on the 15th,[1] four were assigned to High Wood, but one was ditched at the outset. Of the other three, one was set on fire by shells, and the other two lost their bearings and ended up in British lines. One of them was bogged in a shell hole, and the other mistakenly opened fire on men of the London Regiment, killing and wounding some of them.

George stayed on the Somme during those final days of September as the hopeless battle continued and the weather deteriorated, and them he 'tracked up to Ypres' and remained there until the following summer.

---

1   Steven Q. Henriques, in a letter to *The Times*, 15th September 1976, maintained that the late Basil Henriques commanded a tank that 'went into action on the Somme near the village of Morval on September 14th 1916, and he always believed that his tank was the first to fire upon the Germans'.

The transport lines in the Ypres sector, when George arrived in October 1916, were at Dickebusch, a partly wooded area about three miles south-west of the ruined town and four miles due west of Hill 60. It bore that name because it was just sixty metres (about 200 feet) high, and it had helped to screen the German batteries firing on Ypres from the neighbouring ridge to the west of Zandvoord.

Despite the destruction all round him the conditions at Dickebusch were a marked improvement on the Somme. George had a Nissen hut to sleep in and there was cover for the horses.

'But it was no holiday. Jerry shelled us most of the time, and he used a lot of high-velocity shells. They would come over with a high whine and then burst in the air so that they spread their shrapnel all over the place. Whenever there was heavy shelling, especially when going up the line at night, the horses would sort of cling to you. You could feel it - a kind of bond. So it was up to you to understand. They sensed when you were looking after them, and they never panicked no matter how bad the firing got. At this time I was taking supplies every night to Hill 60 and the Bluff sector.'

It was at Hill 60 in April 1915 that the Germans, driven from the hill, had used poison gas for the first time and, on the 5th May, the British forces (the East Surreys) had to withdraw in the face of a fog of asphyxiating gas. The German success in the use of this new weapon meant that the Army was unable to go onward from Ypres, and a planned offensive in the spring of 1916 had had to be postponed because of the need to reinforce the Somme. Instead, an enormous mining operation had been undertaken, with British sappers driving galleries deep beneath the Messines Ridge, which was held by the Germans. Other British miners, with the help of Australians, mined deeply beneath Hill 60, about two-and-a-half miles north-west of the ridge.

It was in preparation for the actions that were to follow that George had been among those moved to the Ypres front to reinforce the supply lines.

The method George had used on the Somme, of watching and timing the enemy salvos and then carefully judging the distance he could safely move, he again employed when taking up supplies from Dickebusch, and quickly earned a reputation for the skill of his operation.

'From Dickebusch I would go down the road to what

they called Cafe Belge corner. I would go as far as I dare, to the last house, before turning right, and then I'd come out about two kilometres the right side of Ypres. From the last house to Cafe Belge corner was a bit open, so I was always careful not to show myself, until I had to make the dash. Jerry shelled that corner at about seven o'clock at night. I remember one night there was a young lad - he wasn't in my battalion or my transport either; I think he was a 21st London chap - and he'd got a cart load of water. Well, he do come down the road, and so I halted him. I told him, "For God's sake don't you go down there. You wait till this lot's over." Well, he said he hadn't got time to wait. "I shouldn't go if I were you," I said, "do you won't reach it." But he wouldn't be ruled by me, and off he went. He'd just got to Cafe Belge corner and, of course - wallop - he copped it. That killed the horses and him too. They were two roan horses he'd got, lovely things they were. He was a silly young fellow.

'A funny thing happened when I was at Dickebusch. About a half dozen of us had to go down to the artillery camp to learn to ride. I thought that was a bit odd, but I didn't say anything. Then when the corporal in charge saw me on a horse, he said: "Well, I don't know what you're here for. There's no need for you to come again. You're all right." He wouldn't believe that I hadn't been in the Army before. Neither would my sergeant at that time - Sergeant Soper. He was a strict man, but he was good. I used to like him. He said: "Well, if you haven't been in the Army, you've had a lot to do with horses, the way you sit on them." "That I have," I said, "practically all my life, I've been messing about with horses".'

It was in the early months of 1917 that George was made a lance-corporal, and this meant he had a 'spare man', Wally Jones, to help him look after the horses, to groom them and clean their harness. This was done methodically and never neglected, in spite of the mud and the shellfire.

In April 1917 George had news of the death of his brother, Morris. He died from wounds, aged 22. The news came in a letter from his sister. Sergeant Soper handed him the letter, remarking that it was urgent. He watched as George read it, and asked: 'Bad news?'

'"Yes, that isn't very good," I said. "My brother has died from

George at the door of the Boxford cottage that was his family home for more than 60 years. (Insert) : George joined the army in May 1915.

Betsy Jane (above) and
David Henry Everett (facing page), George's parents.

The cottages at Bower House Tye. George was born in the centre cottage.

George's cottage garden 'was devoted almost exclusively to growing vegetables and dahlias'.

Polstead Ponds. 'We had to see who could throw stones over the top of the trees into the pond'.

Brewery Farm, Polstead, where George began work on his fourteenth birthday.

Sprott's Farm, Polstead.

wounds." Well, that night I was due to take the transport up with the rations, but the sergeant cancelled it. "You stop here," he said. "You don't want to go up there tonight. I'll put another one on it." I appreciated that. He was a kind man. But that got me thinking again. It's funny how somehow I'd come to accept everything - the bombardment, the gunfire, the mud and the filth, the wounded and the dead. But now it was my own brother, and I thought of my mother again. I knew how it would affect her, and I more or less prayed that I would be spared.'

Undoubtedly George owed his survival in large measure to the skill he displayed in handling his horses under shellfire and his Suffolk wariness and judgement. He nevertheless had some 'narrow squeaks'.

'One night we had to go up with the supplies into the wood. All the telegraph wires in the village were down and, on our way through, the horses got tangled up in them. That took some time, cutting the wires, pulling them aside and disentangling the horses - too long for my liking, with the shells a-coming over. Anyway, we got them disentangled, but to get to the ration dump we had to go down a sunken road. Jerry was shelling it all the time. Somehow he just didn't catch the road, but they were dropping on the top of it.

'I got a bit too close for comfort to one of them. My tin hat was blown off, one of the horses was struck in the nose, and a piece of shell hit the front of the saddle. I was sitting on it at the time, but I didn't see it. I found the splinter afterwards, and threw it away. The horse was all right too. The vet came and stitched the wound, and she didn't seem to be too troubled

'Well, we got to the dump all right - just inside the wood, but someone had to go back and pick up sandbags and a screw of barbed wire - pickets we called them. That was a pretty rough night, and the sergeant-major said to me, "You don't want to trouble about them tonight. Just you get back as quick as you like." "Oh no, I shan't do that," I told him. "I'll pick those sandbags up and bring them back." And so I did. Me and another driver went and fetched them.

'I shall never forget that night. The sergeant-major - I think his name was Rowley - looked at me and said, "Whatever are you back for?" When I told him we'd brought the sandbags and the pickets, he said, "You'd better come down here and have something." So we went down into his dug-out, and I had a tot of rum.

As a matter of fact, I think I had a wee drop too much, because I began to see three or four sergeant-majors. So I thought I'd better push off.

'I don't remember much about getting back that night. The whole sky seemed to be torn apart, and there were explosions everywhere, but any old how we got back in the end.'

On another occasion George thought he had been hit by shrapnel, but it was happily a false alarm. Again it was at night and the Germans were shelling the transport lines to try to prevent supplies being taken to the front.

'One of my mates, Len Smith, and I kept together during the shelling. They were coming everywhere, and the whole ground was throbbing and bouncing with them. When the worst stopped, Len said he'd been hit. He'd got a bit of shrapnel in his arm, and I felt for all the world as though I'd been hit in the right hand. Well, we lay down, and I could just see a glimmer of light from a bell tent. So we crawled towards it, and that turned out to be our first-aid post. When we looked at my hand that wasn't marked at all. So I reckon that was just the vibration of the earth that had caused the sensation. Anyway, I'd been lucky again.'

Throughout May 1917 the British bombardment of enemy positions reached a new intensity. At this stage of the war Britain was outpacing the Germans in the manufacture of guns and shells, and new heavy artillery had been brought into action. German trenches and dug-outs were under almost ceaseless gunfire. The offensive which had been postponed a year previously had now been planned and even rehearsed in great detail. It began on a misty moonlit night shortly after three o'clock. It was the 7th of June.

George's transport lines were then at Oudendhem, just back of Ypres and about a mile from Dickebusch, and that night he took supplies to the front. 'Our battalion lay at the Bluff sector just to the right of Hill 60, and I went up that night with the rations. As I passed the colonel's dug-out someone told me he wanted to speak to me. "Get back as quick as you can tonight," he said, "because things are going to happen. But don't gallop, will you?" I told him I wouldn't do that. I never did. That would have been asking for trouble.

'Well, that was about two o'clock when he spoke to me, and I reckon it was just over an hour later that it happened. The whole sky was ablaze with every colour of the rainbow. There were huge red and orange flares as the mines went up, and the sky was cracking and banging like mad.[1]

'I knew they had been mining under Hill 60 for months, and I'd just got back and was jumping off my horse, when up that went - the hill blown sky-high. That was an almighty explosion that nearly threw me to the ground.'

After this offensive there followed, for George, a period of comparative peace. His unit moved some three miles west to Reninghelst 'for a bit of a rest'. While he was there he saw King George V and Lloyd George during their inspection of troops. Slowly his transport moved down to Vimy. He was there during the visit of the Prince of Wales. 'I thought how very young he looked, younger even than he seemed in the pictures I'd seen in the papers.' Still out of the worst of the action, George, with the same two horses, moved on to Arras, which he remembers for its open square, the Petite Place, flanked by a few remaining buildings, but for the most part a crumbling ruin. 'The sight of rubble and wrecked buildings had become so common you almost didn't notice it.'

By October, George had returned to the Somme, this time to the Bapaume front, and he remained there until driven back by the Germans in their offensive which began on the 21st March 1918. It was a quiet but hard winter of frost and snow. He escaped the frostbite suffered by many of his compatriots in the trenches, but remembers the air as crisp and cold and giving the desolate landscape a curious unreality. The comparative quiet, the unreal peace that snow had spread over the battlefields, was shattered in the spring-like weather of late March.

The nights were moonlit and misty. The mist curled off the slopes of the chalk downs and through the valleys around Bapaume. From early morning on Thursday the 21st March the whole line was pounded by thunderous enemy gunfire. It was the beginning of one of the most extraordinary German assaults of the war. After a storm of shellfire and, in some areas, clouds of gas, men in dense packs of apparently impenetrable depth, poured themselves through the blasted wire entanglements at the British defences. They rolled on in enormous grey waves, falling to the British fire in their thousands. In some sectors heavy British guns had been withdrawn and the infantry had only the support of some field batteries to check the enemy. The chalky land between

---

1 It was estimated afterwards that four million shells were fired by the British artillery that night.

Arras and Bapaume, however, provided many good defensive positions, which enabled British gunners to direct fire selectively at the Germans moving into abandoned ground. But against the sheer weight of numbers thrown into the battle at whatever sacrifice of thousands of lives, it was clear that ultimately the enemy could not be held. There were neither sufficient guns nor sufficient ammunition to put up the kind of curtain of fire that might have held the German infantry back.

George especially recalls one of these March nights, when thin strands of mist curled in the shell-struck, moonlit sky. Men of the 21st, 22nd and 23rd London had already tried to get supplies of rations through to the front lines without success.

'They couldn't get them through because Jerry was a-pounding them so much. As we set out I met a 23rd London chap, and he said, "George, you'll never get through". "Well, we shall have to see," I told him, but I wondered whether this was going to be the night that I copped it. The sound was deafening, and there were shells landing all round us, sending up spouts of earth.

'I had a quartermaster - Mr Beer - going up with me, and we went along a cart-track, leaving a village to our right and crossing the main Arras-to-Bapaume road near a church. I told him he had to go straight across and it was agreed that he should go through with the first limber, and then I would send through the others when I thought it was safe. You had to watch points that night, because the shells were coming thick and fast.

'Well, I watched him go, and as soon as he reached the church he turned left, so that he was going down the main road towards Arras. I reckon he got a little flustered. It was lucky that I saw him, with the help of a bit of moonlight and the flashes of gunfire. So I got the other limbers through as quick as I could, and then I trotted off after Mr Beer.

"You've gone wrong," I shouted at him. "You've got to halt. I reckon you lost your head a bit." And he did look as though he had too. Anyway, we got him turned round, and I trotted off in front, and as I come by the church, I met the ration party. "Where have we got to dump them?" I asked. "Along the road there at the foot of the wood," I was told. So off we went, and I got them all through. As each limber was unloaded I sent it back straight away. I stayed until we'd unloaded the last one, and then I said to Mr Beer, "Come you along, we're ready now." I thought to myself, "So far, so good," but the gunfire that night was the worst

I'd known it, and I could see that he was wondering, too, if we would ever make it back. Any road, we set off, and before we got to the church over come a shell right on the rations. That blew most of them up. But I was lucky. Blast, we were both lucky that night. We got back safely. The horses had been marvellous. They hadn't been worried at all.'

The battle for Bapaume reached a pitch of intensity on the night of Saturday 23rd March, and for two more days the troops around the town fought to hold back the unstoppable concentration of German troops to allow for some ordered retreat. For George the way back was the ten miles down the road to Albert, and by the 25th the Germans had advanced more than half way towards the town. Tanks were deployed down this road to hold back the enemy and to allow heavy guns to be brought back to the line of the Ancre. 'Oh, they were hauling the huge artillery down the road as fast as they could go, and all the time they were under tremendous bombardment from German guns.' The retreat was also threatened by the enemy breakthrough first at Clery and then, on the 25th March, at Maricourt.

The fighting continued incessantly through the day and the moonlit nights.

'The sky, day and night, was full of aeroplanes - British, French and American, and they were dropping bombs on the advancing Jerries and their supply lines. The noise was unbelievable. And he didn't seem to have any answer to the aeroplanes. There wasn't much anti-aircraft action. Even further down the road, where we were, you could see the planes swooping down quite low and you could hear their machine-guns.'

In the early evening of the 26th March grey swarms of German troops swept down the slopes from Orvillers, Pozieres and La Boisselle into the valley of the Ancre and were met by a barrage of machine-gun and rifle fire. Altogether four German divisions attacked Albert, which was held by one British division only, until essential supplies and equipment had been removed from the town. Then the British withdrew, leaving the ruins to be occupied by Germans and subjected to heavy shelling. The enormous loss of life sustained by the advancing armies decided the battle. The Germans had been fought to a standstill and were then to remain in their final lines for months before withdrawing.

Such was the demand for manpower that George again found himself in the trenches at Millencourt, just west of Albert, although he remained in transport and still had the care of his light bay horses, Kitty and Ruby.

'From there you could see Jerry moving about even in the ruins of the church. It was spring and the weather was good, and you somehow felt that it was beginning to end. We were still hammering Jerry with gunfire, and it seemed it couldn't go on like this forever. We all knew he'd lost thousands of men in this advance, and I reckoned there must be a limit to that.'

For George the war was almost over, because although in the remaining months his horse transport was still delivering rations and other supplies to troops in action, he never again had to face the intensity of bombardment that had characterized the German push of March 1918. After the lines west of Albert had been consolidated, he moved up towards the northern sector, but did not become involved in the desperate German thrust from the Lille ridge to capture the Channel ports. This April assault, again launched with an overwhelming superiority of forces, was halted on the 29th April, and by the time George got into the sector the Germans were already beginning to withdraw from the lands they had briefly conquered before being pushed back through Lille in the autumn.

Through that summer, George says that he and his comrades had a hunch that the war was coming to an end.

'We weren't told anything. We didn't hear any news. But it wasn't such rough going for us. There wasn't such heavy shelling, and I just had the feeling that there wasn't much longer to go.

'One summer's day, I was unloading my horses at Lillers.[1] station, and as I was standing there I saw in the train another Boxford man - a chap called Chase Gunn. He was going home on leave. The coincidence of seeing a bloke from my own village out there made me think about home again, and I began to wonder if I'd ever get there. I'd just given up the leave due to me so that the sergeant - Sergeant Rance was his name - could go home. He'd got some domestic trouble, I think. The next time I was to see Chase was in the village after the war. He became a bus driver for Eastern Counties.

'Well, when the sergeant came back, the full corporal -

---

1 Although the German April offensive established a line just beyond Merville, it never reached either Bethune or Lillers to the south.

Corporal Shaler - wanted to go home on leave, and I had to go in front of the Colonel, and he asked me if I'd mind giving up my leave again. "I don't mind doing it," I said, "although we're not the best of friends." I don't know why he took against me. I'd never done him any harm. "But," I told the Colonel, "if I keep putting my leave off perhaps I shall catch one, and then I shan't have any leave at all."

'"Well, if you do it this time," the Colonel said, "I promise that you'll be the first to go when he comes back." He was true to his word, but by then the armistice had already been signed.'

It was in the last days of the war, after years in which the experience of death had become commonplace, that an incident occurred which moved George profoundly at the time and the memory of which has stayed with him ever since. It happened on the Lille front.

'One day a fresh-faced young lad - he looked no more than fourteen - asked me what it was like up the line. He said he had to go up that night. I told him not to garp about looking for Jerry, because the Germans would be able to see him anyway. I told him not to volunteer for anything, but just to do what was asked of him. Well, he say he was a bit worried. You see, he'd lost his father and his brother, and there was only his mother left. If anything should happen to him he didn't know how she would manage. "How old are you then?" I asked him. "Eighteen," he said.

'He was a nice young lad. I felt sorry for him, I did. Well, that night he went up the line, and so did I - taking supplies as usual. And I went up the next night too. I complained to the sergeant, "But I went up last night." "Yes, and you're a-goin' up tonight," he say. And so I did.

'Well, when we'd unloaded the supplies, the sergeant up the line said to me, "You've got fourteen tonight, George." You see, we used to take supplies up, and bring the dead back.

'The very first dead soldier I saw was that young boy. That was the first time I ever cried during the war. That was the last too.

'Not long after that the armistice was signed. We'd got beyond Lille then. I shall never forget going through the arched gateway of Lille at night. People were still cheering. Suddenly I was stopped by the sound of an English woman's voice. Soon she recognized my accent, and told me she used to live in Suffolk. She said there were still more than thirty English people in Lille who had somehow managed to survive.'

She told him horrible stories of thousands of women (one estimate put it at fifty thousand) taken from Lille and two other towns.

And she told me, "Don't you touch any women here. Six thousand of them have got syphilis from the Germans." Next day the C.O. gave the same order. "We'll provide for your needs later," he said. And they did. They sent up some clean girls from Paris. Any man who wanted one had to get a metal disc from the C.O, and that entitled you to have one.

'We'd got through Lille on our way to Brussels by the time the armistice was signed. On Sunday the 10th November, the transport officer say to me, "Can you keep a secret?" I told him I reckoned I could, and then he said that the armistice was going to be signed the next day. "Well, we'll have to be careful tonight," I said, because we had still got to take the rations up to the front. That was a funny feeling then, knowing that the next day it would all be over, and yet that night you'd still got to go up to the front, and you could still get killed. That made you feel a bit uneasy. Anyway, that was a quiet night, and we got back all right.

'The next morning, we were on our way back - we were the 47th Division, and were being relieved by the 74th - when a despatch rider rode up and told us the armistice had been signed. There was a moment of silence, and then we all burst out cheering. Suddenly you felt safe. That made you almost light-headed with relief. I thought of my mother.

'It was soon after that I had my leave. Before I went, I had to go before the Colonel again, and he told me that he was sending me on leave, and that he would make me a full corporal. And he did.'

George's promotion was soon to be followed by another recognition of his services. He had been recommended for a decoration on a number of occasions; twice his name had gone forward for the DCM (Distinguished Conduct Medal) but no award had been made. He returned from his leave early in December, and he and his mate, Ginger King, found a billet with a miner and his wife at the village of Allouagne. One night they were celebrating with French soldiers in a nearby inn. He had just changed uniforms with one of the Frenchmen, when a runner came into the inn and yelled out, "Is Corporal Everett here.?"

'He looked a bit puzzled when I told him I was Corporal

Everett. He said I'd got to go down to headquarters, and when I asked him what for, all he said was, "You'll know when you get there." I said, "Well, you'll have to wait." I think I was three-parts cut. Anyway, me and the other chap went into a room and changed back into our own uniforms, and then I went with a runner back to headquarters.

That's when I was given a ribbon for the Military Medal. The quartermaster said to me, "Corporal Everett I want to see that on your tunic in the morning." But that wasn't on there, I can tell you. I didn't feel well enough.

'I never knew exactly what I got it for. Of course they told me at the time, but I reckon I was too far gone to remember. I suppose it was for getting the rations up to the front at sometime or other.'

George's last months in the Army were spent in the billet that he and Ginger King had found at Allouagne. This was in the coal-mining area of Bethune. The German advance in the previous April had been fought to a standstill just north of Bethune, and in this part of the northern French coalmines, the miners had gone on working under perpetual aerial bombardment and long-distance artillery fire. The coal they had extracted under these conditions provided relief both to British mines and the ships carrying their coal.

The small house of this mining family, with its well-scrubbed brick floor and strip of carpet in front of the fire, had a homely familiarity.

George recalls the wife as 'a very clean, nice little woman, who kept everything spick and span. There were two children, a boy called Vernon, and a little girl whose name I can't remember, although I often used to nurse her. She was a nice little kid, and I wondered if I would ever have one like her of my own.'

This reflection almost came true in an unexpected way. A girl from Bruay, a town about four miles south-east of Bethune, came searching the ranks for the father of her child. She had named him as Len Smith, one of George's mates in his transport section. Apparently she and Len had met when the regiment had been in the district earlier in the war, but George had not been with them on that occasion.

'Now the trouble was that Len and I were very much alike. In fact we were often mistaken for brothers. Well, when she came round, the Colonel decided to put us on parade, and let her go along the ranks to pick out the man she reckoned was her child's father. That so happened Len was in hospital at this time. Anyway, she come along the ranks, and she do pick me out. "That's him," she said. That gave me a rum old feeling I can tell you.'

George protested that he had never met the girl, and when she declared that his name was Len Smith, the Colonel came to the rescue and showed her George's passbook.

During these few weeks at the end of his Army career George formed a romantic attachment of his own, with a girl that he met at his billet. She was a niece, who lived with another uncle two or three miles away. Her name was Marie, and George remembers her as 'a pretty, dark-haired girl, a bit younger than me, and a Roman Catholic.'

The first time she came to the household, it was evident that both George and Ginger King were eyeing her admiringly. George seized the advantage, however, and said quietly, 'I'm a-going to take her home tonight'. The girl, who both understood and spoke English, had overheard him.

'What did you say?' she asked him.

George boldly repeated his intention, and the girl offered no objection. To a countryman, whose only means of getting from place to place had mostly been on foot, the two or three miles to the farmstead that she shared with her uncle was no hardship. George walked her home, and that was the first of many meetings. The relationship developed quickly, and the pair became fond of each other. Marie and her uncle had somehow managed to keep their small farm going throughout the war, so apart from any attraction they had for each other, George and Marie shared a common background and upbringing. They both knew about cultivating the land.

George evidently got on well with her uncle too, because before long he was discussing the possibility of the pair of them getting married. When he learned of George's own farming background, he suggested that, after George had been demobbed, he should return and help them both to farm their holding. If the young couple married, then the uncle was content to make the farm over to George. It was the offer of a new life with a young woman he had undoubtedly become very fond of, and George considered the future, but he considered it in that wary, practical Suffolk way of his.

He had often thought he would like a farm of his own - to be his own master - and here was the opportunity, albeit in a foreign country.

'Well, I thought about it. And she was a nice girl, and I was fond of her, 'tis true, but everything seemed so very uncertain at that time. I mean, I'd just been through one war and was lucky to be alive, and I wondered if there might not be another war break out at any time. I hadn't got a feeling that all was settled. And I didn't want to be out there in the middle of it if that was all going to happen again. I was English, and she was French, and I didn't know how I'd settle down in France. Then she was a Roman Catholic, too. So in the end I decided against it. I've often thought about it since, and wondered what might have happened. Where would I have been in 1939?'

So George left the little farmstead in northern France to Marie and her uncle, and in February 1919 he returned to England. He was demobbed at Thetford, in Norfolk, on the 11th February. He returned to his parents at number six Butchers Lane, Boxford, the small cottage where he was to live for the next sixty years.

He never wrote to Marie, or made any attempt to get in touch with her again. The war was over. The brief relationship had come to an end. George's new life was back in his native Suffolk.

15
'I won't be tied'

The new life was really to be the old life all over again. Within weeks George was back working on the land just as he had been before the war. He had parted from his horses, Kitty and Ruby, the day before he left France. It was an unemotional parting - a pat on the neck, and that was that. George was never to see them again, and he heard nothing of their fate. There would be other horses in Suffolk.

Boxford seemed quiet and drab. 'But there was a feeling of relief. Nothing would ever be the same again. There'd never be another war. I think most people hereabouts were sure that we had seen the war to end all wars.'

There was widespread unemployment. 'There weren't any factories for the lads to go to. We were country boys and we relied on the land. You had to eat a lot of humble pie to keep a job in those days.'

In fact, the cost of living had risen about 125 per cent compared with pre-war days. Boxford people were hard up. The few local tradespeople, the farmers, and the building firm of Kingsbury were the main sources of employment.

Kingsburys had been in the village since the sixteenth century. There's an entry in the churchwardens' accounts, dated 1540, with a note of money paid to a member of the family for work done on the church. Kingsburys, however, had lived in the neighbourhood very much longer. The family was established in Cornard, a few miles away, in 1369, and two Kingsburys moved to Boxford during the reign of Henry VIII. By 1630 three brothers and their families sailed for the New World with John Winthrop, and one of the brothers, Joseph, built the first church in New England.

The firm employed as many men as they could, but so soon after the war there was a limited amount of building being done. Although later, as the industry expanded, so did the firm of

104

Kingsbury. Then they were really the mainstay of village employment. At one time they had over a hundred men on their books.'[1]

The village had lost thirty-eight of its men in the war. George's younger brother, Morris, was one of them, and among the others were members of many old village families bearing names like Grimwood, Munson, King, Rice, Godden, Whymark and Elmer. (By comparison seven were killed in the second world war.)

George's brother Bill - the eldest of the family - was still living at home. He had been unfit for military service and had worked on the land throughout the war. His sister Mary, called Polly in the family, was in service, and Ruth, his elder sister, was married. Arthur, the third to be born, had also survived the war, but was unable to settle in Suffolk afterwards, and left to find work near Chelmsford in Essex. His younger brother, Charlie, joined the Army just after the war and served for a time in India, and after that he became a nurse at Colchester.

'All the family had nicknames except me. My brother Bill was called Kipper. I think it was because sometimes, instead of saying "give me" or "gimme", he would say "kipper". Jack's nickname was Truncheon, but I don't know why. And Arthur was called Quilter or Kilter. That came about because Sir Cuthbert Quilter was the local Conservative candidate in an election, and Eaton Armstrong was the Liberal. The foreman on the farm where Arthur worked asked him who he was going to vote for, and Arthur said he'd vote for Kilter.

'My brother Morris, who was killed in the war, was nicknamed Taggle or Tagel, but how he got the name I don't know. And Charlie, the younger one, was called Shady. I suppose he got that in the Army. Before that he was sometimes called Spencer. That might have been because of the way he talked about Mr Churchill. He studied politics more than the rest of us. But I never got called anything, except "Garge".'

Before being demobbed George had voted for the first time - in the election of 1918. He had not been particularly interested in politics, 'but enticed by the London chaps, I voted Labour, for a man called Hicks'.

Mr J R Hicks in fact stood as Agriculturist/Farmers' candidate, and came bottom of the poll on a turnout of less than half the electorate, in what was then the Sudbury division of West

1 Sadly, the firm went into liquidation in 1984.

Suffolk. Apart from George's vote he got another 389, and the seat was won, as was the tradition then, by the Liberal, Mr S G Howard, with a majority over his Conservative opponent, Mr R G Proby, of 910 votes. But George had no great passion for politics.

'I used to take things casually, weigh them up for myself. I mean, you weren't forced to be led by someone else, were you? I was never led away like that. I'd got my own opinion, and I voted according to that.'

The village, in fact, had a fairly strong Liberal tradition. Immediately after the war, however, it struck George as being somewhat exhausted by the years of conflict; it had become inured to the shortages of war time.

George returned bearing his certificate of employment. He had ended the war as a full corporal, but the document still described him as lance-corporal. It read: 'Certificate of Employment during the war. Regimental No. 722937, L/Cpl George Albert Everett, transport driver, described as farmer before enlisting. "This NCO is a thoroughly good horseman with a practical knowledge of horses. As a driver in the transport section he has always had one of the best teams." The object of this certificate is to assist the soldier in obtaining employment on his return to civil life.'

In fact George had no difficulty in finding work, but a strange obstinacy ensured that he did not take advantage of the recommendation that he was a thoroughly good horseman.

He returned to the small cottage where his parents lived in Butchers Lane, Boxford. It was hard on the lane's edge, at the end of a row of timber-framed, stud and plaster dwellings, with their first floors oversailing sufficiently to keep the base of the buildings dry. There were no foundations; it was constructed on an oak frame, and had stood there with its companions since about 1490 or 1500, when it may have been a weaver's cottage or even a shop - part of the narrow medieval street. It was lit by oil lamps, and the water came from a well at the end of the garden. His father was still working as a farm labourer, and his mother, looking just a little more frail, continued to keep the home spotless, and managed on the minimum of resources.

A letter was waiting for George from his pre-war employer, the farmer, Mr Edward Lilley.

His mother told him, 'Mr Lilley says he wants you to go back.'

'I suppose he do,' George answered, and remembered that he was entitled to a month's leave. He hadn't been home more than a day or so, however, before Mr Lilley called on him.

'I told him I was going to have my leave first. "I haven't had a bed to lie on lately," I said, "and I want a bit of a rest." Of course, he went on about being busy and all that. He came again the next week, but I still said "No", and then he called again at the end of the week. "Oh, all right then," I said, "I shall have to come." So I did, and I'd had a fortnight at home.'

George went back to the farm as a day-man, that's to say an ordinary farm labourer who was expected to do almost any job about the farm. He was, however, very soon offered the job of horseman.

Before the war, it was only the horsemen who were paid a regular wage; the day-men drew no money if the weather made work impossible. The Corn Production Act of 1917, however, gave the farmer guaranteed prices and fixed a minimum wage - it was then 25 shillings (£1.25) a week - for farm workers. Hundreds of men returning from the war joined the farm-workers' union. George was among them. But not everywhere was the guaranteed wage observed. George remembers in a wet week before Christmas working no more than four hours and taking home three shillings and sixpence (17 1/2p).

The offer of the job of horseman would have meant that George was the top workman on the farm. He rejected it, not because he was afraid of responsibility - he had borne that cheerfully enough during the war - but through a mixture of obstinacy, pride and independence.

'He wanted me to take the horses, get married, and live in his cottage at Sprotts Farm. I said, "No thanks, I shall never be tied to a master. No, I shan't. And another thing," I said, "where do you think I've got the money to take a woman and make a home?" I'd never had anything out of the land. I went into the Army and I hadn't had anything out of that either ... well, only just the gratuity money they allowed us. Twenty-six pounds, I think it was. So I said, "No, I'm not going to get married like that, Mr Lilley." He told me I needn't worry. He'd make a home for me. "Oh no," I said, "no you don't. Oh no, I'm not going to tie myself to you, not to no one."

'Well, I heard he'd also got another man who'd take the horses and live there. So I told him, "If you want to get rid of me, you can." "No," he say, "I don't want to get rid of you." But I told him, "You might as well be frank and admit you've got another man to take the horses." "Oh, and how do you know that? Who told you that?" I said, "The man did himself. He came and told me." And he had. He'd said to me, "If he's going to sack you, George, I shan't take the job. I wouldn't try to do another chap out of a job." I said to him, "You take it, and I'll get something else. I'm not worried." But he wouldn't do that. So Mr Lilley said, "No, I'll find you another job. I'm not going to get rid of you. Only I'd really like you to take the horses and live here." So I had to tell him again, "No, I'll never do that," I said, "I'm not going to live under no master."

'Of course I'd thought about it, on the quiet, you know. But the wage wasn't anything. I was only getting thirteen bob (65p) a week, though that should have been more. You couldn't save to get a home together on that, could you? I didn't want him to buy me a home and plump me in there. You were tied as soon as you did that, and I didn't want to be tied. I don't think that's right to be tied. I thought to myself, "I can't take a woman. I'm not going to tie myself to a woman and more or less half starve, the both of us." Well, there weren't enough for one to live on let alone two. I know how we'd had to pinch when I was young, and I thought to myself, "That'll never happen to me." And that's the reason I never got married. The wage wasn't good enough. And so my mother stood first. I thought to myself, "She's had a rough time, bringing us up, and if I do keep single, then I can help her." And that's what I did. Of the thirteen bob I was getting, I gave my mother seven bob (35p) a week for board. And she always got that. I used to hang on to my six bob as near as I could, and then if that were a wet day and I had to be at home and lost money, she would always have her seven shillings. Of course you couldn't spend much on yourself. Still, there weren't nothing much to spend it on.

'My father, just after the war, poor old chap, he was not too well, and they don't want you on the land when you're getting on. He never had regular work. And times were bad. He'd get an occasional job, threshing perhaps, a day or two a week. So I hung on, and more or less kept them going.

'I give up all hopes of marriage after that. I mean, if you get married you're liable to have two or three children, which I should have liked because I like children, I always have, but I thought about what I'd had to go through when I was young, and I said to myself, "I'll never follow in my father's footsteps. No, I'll just forget it." And that's what I did.

'Of course I had girl friends, quite a few. They were mostly Boxford girls. But one of them lived in Edwardstone, and then one of the Boxford girls went to live there too. I used to take them home. One night I'd be out with one, and another night I'd be with the other. Nobody took it very seriously, but they were happy old times, although we didn't have much money to handle. But anyhow we made our own enjoyment.'

The war had not brought any significant changes in farming ways to this part of Suffolk. The methods of cultivation were mostly those that had developed through the centuries and had their historic links with the Middle Ages. The real agricultural revolution was yet to come. It was still a rare sight to see a tractor on a farm, and it was going to be almost another ten years before George began to plough with a tractor. Mr Lilley remained faithful to horses, and the labour force was still calculated on the basis of about three men for every hundred acres.

One of the first jobs George did on his return to the land was muck spreading. There were usually ten or twelve loads of manure to the acre, and by now there was a manure drill to help with the task. This was barrel-shaped with a ribbed plate at the bottom and a spout each side, and as the drill was drawn across the field, the muck was pushed out of the spouts.

'Well, that was all right on a still day. But if that was windy you copped it, I can tell you. And that still had to be spread with a fork afterwards.

'I can tell you another story about muck spreading - of a different kind. That was in the twenties, probably 1921, and I was growing some sweet peas in the garden. Well, I used to have a bumby[1] at the end of the garden that I put all the swills and slops into. A man came round from time to time to empty the closet, you know. So I asked him if he'd put a couple of buckets of the night soil into the bumby. So he did. Well, I asked old Mr Stacey, who was the gardener at Groton Hall, if I could plant sweet peas in that. He said, no, that would burn them. "All right," I said, "I'll be ruled by you." But I weren't wholly ruled by him. I planted some of my sweet peas in the ordinary earth, and then I dug a trench, tipped

---

1   Suffolk dialect: a place for the contents of an outdoor privy. Forby puts it charmingly: 'There is commonly a *bumby* behind the little concealed retreat at the corner of the garden.'

some of the night soil into it, and I planted the other sweet peas in that.

'They did a treat. They come up much better than the others. Mr Stacey come and he looked at those in the ordinary earth, and he said he couldn't understand why they hadn't done as well as the others. So I told him they were the ones I'd been ruled by him over, and the others, I told him, I'd planted in the night soil. "Well," he say, "thas a rummin'."

'D'you know, one day Aggie Kemball - she was one of the daughters of Charlie Kemball, who lived at Kemball House on the corner of the lane - looked over the wall and she saw my lovely sweet peas, and she asked if she could have some for the flower show. I told her she could, but blast, when I next looked out in the garden, they'd all gone. Not a bloom to be seen anywhere. Next day, you won't believe it, she was selling bunches of them. But she never give me a penny for them. Not that I mind.'

After his muck spreading on the farm, George's next job was hedging and brushing. It was essential to brush round the field before ploughing could begin. Many of the hedgerows had obviously existed for hundreds of years, and periodically they needed thinning and cleaning and the dead wood removed.

Laying a hedge was a skilled and hard task. First, the lower part of the hedge was cut free of weeds, old brambles, dead wood and any other extraneous growth. This was done with an implement like a bill-hook, and known to George as a rip. It had a wooden handle and a barely curved blade with a hook-like end to it. Usually the trees in the hedgerow were ten or twelve feet high before hedging was done. Then the long branches or shoots were half-cut at an angle, laid flat and woven one into the other. It was important not to cut them through, because they had to continue growing, and the whole purpose of the operation was to thicken and strengthen the hedgerow. The straighter shoots were left standing upright to allow the others to be woven between them. Sometimes posts were also staked into the ground. The weaving operation was known as pleating or plashing.[1] Tusser, in his *February Husbandry* says: 'Cut vines and osier - plash hedge of enclosure'.

---

1 It is also sometimes called pleaching, although this word is used more in Norfolk than Suffolk. It is referred to in some lines in *Much Ado About Nothing*:

'And bid her steal into the pleached bower,
Where honeysuckles, ripen'd by the sun,
Forbid the sun to enter.'

George was more often concerned with brushing and gap-stopping, which was a more primitive way of laying a hedge.

'You'd got to trim out the bottoms of hedges because during the summer that grow, and bits of branches and brambles and things run out into the field. Well, that would get in the way of the horse and the ploughman. So you had to cut all that out. We called it brushing.[1] I used to like that. But you needed good tough leather gloves on your hands, otherwise you'd be torn to bits. I mean apart from the brambles there'd be sharp pieces of wood as thick as your thumb. Sometimes I had to lay a fence into the hedge. Well, first I'd get hold of some thorn. It didn't matter if that were blackthorn or whitethorn. There was bound to be some of it nearby that I'd already cut out. Then I'd put in these thorn stakes. You sort of mocked[2] them - put one one side and one the other. Then I'd fill in between with the stuff I'd cut, and the mocked stakes would keep it from blowing out. That was a rough old way of laying a hedge, and we called it gap-stopping.

'That was a healthy life, but you'd got to put up with all sorts of weather in the winter if you wanted to earn a crust. We had to work with overcoats on when it was bad, 'tis true, and perhaps with a bag over your shoulders to keep off the rain. But you'd still get wet through.

'Of course that's different now. You don't see much brushing or hedge-laying these days. A lot of farmers just root them out, even the hedges next to the roads, or at best a hedge-cutter comes along and just hacks them through, leaving them all torn and jagged. That don't look very good, and that isn't very good, I reckon. Then they root out the hedges in the fields to make one big open space, and I think that's where some of them have gone wrong, because if you've got a big old hedge up that's a wind-break, and what's more if there's a bit of mildew about that'll catch it. Of course today I know they're farming for the combine. But ripping out all the hedges has got rid of a lot of the birds, and they used to destroy the pests. Why, the hedgerows would be throbbing with song something wonderful. Oh yes, those old hedges were full of birds, but do you know I haven't even seen a yellow-hammer down this lane for years. I think this spraying business has done away with a lot of them. I've an idea that's why you don't

1 In some parts of Suffolk called flashing, because the rip was also known as a flash hook.
2 Not given by Moor, Forby or Claxton, but George says it was the word used locally, meaning to stagger.

see so many coveys of partridges about too. And I can't remember when I last saw a barn owl, for that matter. there used to be scores of them. In the old barns you'd see a hole left in the gable end so an owl could get into the barn. Farmers knew how useful owls were. They killed off the rats and mice. But a lot of the old farm buildings have been pulled down and new ones put up, and you don't see any owl holes in those. They don't look as good either.'

George didn't stay long with his old master. By May 1920 the wages had gone up - thanks to the Corn Production Act - to £2 a week. The figure was resented by many local farmers, who regarded the Act as a mixed blessing. They got a guaranteed price for their corn but at the cost of higher wages and a farm-workers' trade-union movement that was growing in strength.

'Well, Mr Lilley moaned and groaned. He said he couldn't pay £2 a week. He couldn't afford it. "I'm afraid," he said, "you'll have to find something else." "All right," I said, "I will. If you can't afford to keep me I'm not coming here to be moaned and groaned at." I didn't know what else I was going to do. It wasn't easy to get work in those days, but I wasn't going to let him see that I was worried. I took that £2 for one week, that's all, and then I got notice.

'That wasn't so funny at home then. There wasn't much coming in, with my father only doing odd jobs now and again. I thought about the war and all those times on the Somme when I wondered if I'd live through it. Now I was back home again, and nothing seemed much better than before.

'I remembered what I'd thought about when I was around twenty ... being a policeman. I should have liked to join the police force then. But the war came along and put a stop to that idea.

'I suppose really it would have been a way of escaping, although I didn't think of it like that at the time. But now I thought I'd try again. That was a cleaner life, and you handled a bit more money, and there was a little pension at the end of it. I suppose that was more secure, and I liked the uniform. They looked smart fellows. Suddenly that was my ambition again - to be a policeman. I was just the right height too. So I went up to Ipswich Borough Force, and I saw the sergeant there.

'He asked me when I'd been demobbed, and said, "You should have come here then, mate. We were looking for men then, but I've got a hundred on the waiting list now. I'm afraid you've left it too long."

'Blast, I drove that too late, I did. I was really disappointed. I'd set my heart on it. I was twenty-seven, and that would have been a new life. But that's no good feeling sorry for yourself. Mind you, I don't think I'd want to be a policeman today. They don't get enough protection. Criminals nowadays think nothing of knifing a policeman or shooting him.

'I don't know what I would do if I were a young man today. Farming would still be a temptation, 'tis true. But you've really got to have a bit of money behind you to do that. That's a nice healthy life, but that was hard work in my time. I should never do it at the price I used to, that's certain. If I was young again, I think I should want to find something different.'

It was May 1920, and George was out of work. The immediate post-war boom had so far kept unemployment down to reasonable levels, but already there were signs that conditions were worsening. By the end of 1920 there were 858,000 unemployed, and by the spring of the following year the figure had risen to well over one and a half million.

George was to find no regular work until November 1920.

16
Ghosts

At Christmas 1920 George had his first experience of the 'supernatural'. Although he has a practical mind and a common-sense attitude to events, and is sceptical about most country superstitions, the sudden occurence of the inexplicable is, for him, something to be accepted. The ghostly is, in fact, taken for granted. It's not a matter of belief or disbelief. Explanations are not sought. Some things just happen, and that's that.

His area of Suffolk has its share of ghostly phenomena. In one lane at Polstead, which twists down from the rectory[1] monks are said to walk from time to time. But they had never disturbed George. It was however a walking ghost that George met that Christmas.

He had been to a family party at his aunt's, Mrs Woods, at Edwardstone, just over a mile north from his home in the centre of Boxford.

'It wasn't pitch black, but it was a very dark night, so you couldn't distinguish things clearly, but of course after a while your eyes adjust, don't they?

'Well, I left the house by myself, shut the gate behind me and walked down the road. There were fields on either side of me. I didn't catch it up and it didn't catch me up either. Suddenly it appeared right beside me. It was a woman, I could tell that, although I couldn't really see what kind of age she was. She seemed to be wearing a little round hat and a cape, and wasn't much over five feet tall.

'So I began talking to her. I can't think what it was I said

---

1 Polstead Rectory was sold by the Church Commissioners in 1979 after Margo Foster, the wife of the recently appointed Revd Hayden Foster, experienced the sensation of being suffocated or strangled in one of the bedrooms, and had heard screaming. The story was widely reported in both the local and the national press in 1978. The haunting was well-known in the village, and there had been previous attempts at exorcism. Mr Foster and his wife left. The property is now a private residence.

to her. But the only sound was the sound of my boots on the road. There wasn't even a rustle from her.

'I can't say I felt frightened. Things like that happen, I suppose. Some people see them and some don't. I'd never seen her before, and I've never seen her since. I think I was really rather pleased that I'd seen something like that. It certainly didn't worry me.

'I suppose we'd been walking together for three or four minutes, and then she just disappeared.

'Shortly afterwards I caught up with my father and asked him where my brother Bill was. "Oh, he must be home by now," father said. "Well, I wonder who I've been talking to?" I said. He looked at me. "I don't know," he say, "some woman, probably." "Well, that was a woman," I told him, "but I never got no answer from her. She just disappeared." "Oh," he say, "I thought so." I reckon he'd seen her too, but he never mentioned any more about her. He had never been the kind of man to talk much about anything like that. I suppose he thought, when we were children, it would frighten us.

'But he did tell me a rum old story once. That was about the time he was courting my mother and she was living at Bower House Tye. He always had a walking stick with him. You needed one if you were walking on the roads in those days. Well, every time he got near to Tills Farm - that was a little farm just off the road - that walking stick would be pulled out of his hand. He'd stop and pick it up and go a little further. Then that would be pulled out of his hand again.

'I've even heard my mother refer to it. She used to say to him, "That's a funny thing, when you go past there, you can't hold your stick." And he would say, "That is, yes that is." But he wouldn't say any more. I don't know if he ever saw anything. If so he never told anyone. He knew we children had to go up and down that road, and I suppose he thought that would make us nervous.

'I've been past there many times, of course, with sticks and without them, but nothing's ever happened to me.

'You know, they do say that here in Butchers Lane, where I live, there's a ghostly horse that go galloping up and down the lane from time to time. Well, you do hear funny noises now and again, 'tis true, but I've never seen the beast.'

At Groton Hall, an old and rambling house about a mile and

a half from Boxford, George maintains that it is commonly said locally that a horse can be heard going up and down the stairs; and it was one night when returning from Groton towards Edwardstone Park that George had his other ghostly experience.

'I'd been up as far as Edwardstone rectory with a young woman that night. I was coming back alone when I saw a figure in the field alongside me. That stayed level with me for a long time. It was a man. I suppose he could have been a poacher, but I don't think so. He was just walking along the field level with me. Then suddenly, just as we got to the Edwardstone memorial, he disappeared. I was looking at him at the time, and he just went.'

One of the pubs that George has frequented throughout his life is the old coaching inn at Boxford, The Fleece. It has a nice eighteenth-century frontage and a classical doorway with Ionic columns. But behind all that is an old timber-framed building dating from the fifteenth century. It would be surprising if it didn't have its own ghost story. Sure enough, it is supposed to be haunted by a mob-capped young woman of pleasant disposition. A visitor in 1977 claimed to have seen her.

'I've been in that pub a few times,' George says, 'but I've never seen her. My own experiences were only those two at Edwardstone, but I'm sure enough about those.'

17
Threshing and Sawing

Threshing the corn on the farms of West Suffolk was invariably done by a local contractor rather than by the farmer himself, and for the next six years George worked for one of them - Harry Rice. He was a hard-working man who had built his own business from scratch, and was well-liked by the men who worked for him because he behaved like one of them. Only occasionally did the strength of character that had enabled him to make his own way in the world emerge to show the man as the boss. He was tall, lithe and strong. His weathered face had a thick moustache, fashionable at the time, and George remembers him as inevitably shirt-sleeved and waist-coated as he worked with his traction engines. He undoubtedly had a feel for them, and he knew everything about them. 'They were lovely engines he had.'

At that time he had two. The first one he bought well before the 1914-1918 war and when George was still a lad. They were both Burrell steam engines, made by Charles Burrell of Ixworth. Later Mr Rice acquired a third traction engine, built by Garretts of Leiston. From his home on Polstead Heath he would undertake threshing for most of the farms in the neighbourhood. The traction engines were used not only to drive the threshing machine but also to transport it from farm to farm.

'He knew what he was about did Harry Rice. I've known him when the weather was just right - nice and dry - draw into the stackyard, set the machine, and we'd be threshing in twenty minutes. That was quick. Oh, he was a good chap. He had a straight eye, and that was important, because you'd got to have your drum standing level.'

Some wheat was threshed in the summer, after harvest, for seed. So, very often, were oats and beans and peas. After that, the threshing machines were at their busiest in the winter, when the barley was threshed. Finally, there were bound to be a few farmers who left a stack or two of wheat until the end of April or May.

The Burrell engine would burn just over three hundred-weight of coal a day, and sometimes it would take more than a day to thresh a single stack, if it was a large one.

'After the first day's threshing, you'd bank up when you knocked off at night, damp everything down, so there was not much air getting to the boiler. Then you relied on the head horseman next morning. He would pull up the ash pan, give it a bit of draught, and put a little coal on. Then by the time you got there at six o'clock you'd have about twenty or thirty pounds of steam. Once you'd just got it moving and the wheels turning, you'd be surprised how the steam used to gather, if you'd got a feeder who would just drindle[1] in the corn. I've done that hundreds of times, slow and steady. Once you'd got eighty pounds pressure, you could go, and if that got up to a hundred and twenty pounds, you were well away. You didn't want it higher than that.'

The Burrell engine George describes as a 'lovely quiet engine. Providing you drindled in the sheaves even and flat, you hardly knew that was a-going, that was so quiet. If you pitched the sheaves into the drum, then of course that would knock.'

A good man on the drum would always scatter the sheaves evenly across the surface, otherwise a lot of corn would be lost with the straw. Moreover, if the straw was needed for thatching, it was important to feed the sheaves in evenly and flat, otherwise the straw would get broken.

When the corn was fed from the stack into the drum at the top of the threshing machine, rotating beaters separated the ears, and the straw was borne away by revolving combs. The corn dropped on to a riddle which separated the heavier chaff; the lighter chaff was blown away, and the grain fell to a hopper beneath. From here it was borne up by an elevator to the spout from which the corn was sacked.

'It was a dirty old job. Many a time I've been feeding the drum, and when you take the roof off the stacks, the rats jump out at you. Sometimes they'd jump on to you and then fall off into the

---

1 Suffolk dialect. As a verb: to trickle away. As a noun: a small stream trickling along the ground, or a roadside channel for water; also a drill or channel for sowing seeds. Claxton gives an additional meaning: to dawdle, and Moor says the word is sometimes heard figuratively: 'He is the drindlest man I ever did business with'.- a slow man. George frequently uses the word as a verb meaning to feed something slowly, evenly and gently.

drum on to the beaters. Well, there'd be bits of mice and rats thrown all over the place. You'd get splashed with the blood, and the stench was horrible. And there was the chaff flying around, getting stuck to you with your sweat, and up your nostrils. Sometimes I've ended up black as a hat.'

Later in life George developed a skin cancer on his face. This necessitated an operation that removed most of one ear, and the regular treatment of some skin sores.

'I've often wondered if that didn't all begin from that flying chaff and muck when I was feeding the threshing drum.

'As for the vermin, well that wasn't so bad if the mice and rats were down in the stack. Then, of course, they wouldn't jump off, but just run out. We would spread a thick chicken-mesh round the area we were working so they couldn't easily escape. Then you could cop them one, or if the farmer had got dogs around, they'd get them. Now and again there'd hardly be a rat or a mouse to be found. Then you could be sure there were weasels in the stack. We'd always do our best to see that they escaped.

'At one farm we went to there was a funny old boy. He was stacking the straw, and he had another chap to help him. The old boy was a bit religious. He turned to the other fellow, and he said, "Geoffrey, do you know in a thousand years' time, you and me will be stacking this straw again?" Geoffrey looked at him very bewildered, and then he say, "Well, we shall be a couple of rum-lookin' old B's then, sha'n't we?"

'Of course the old traction engine would come in useful to heat up your tea. I always brought a bottle of cold tea with me, and there was a place each side of the engine where you could stick the bottle and warm it up. That would almost boil if you left it there long enough.

'But there wasn't a lot of money attached to that game. Sometimes you could earn a few extra shillings, but if that was a bit wet, the farmers wouldn't open the stack enough. We averaged £2 a week at the most.'

It was in 1921 that farm workers' wages came tumbling down. The summer was long and hot. In some parts of Suffolk there was no rain from March to October, and the corn was stunted, but in the Boxford area there was a break in the weather on the 18th August with a violent and torrential thunderstorm. At the time George was threshing wheat out in the field at the nearby village of Shelley.

'On that day I was the sacker, and I was sacking the corn at the back of the drum when the whole sky darkened and cracked with thunder. The clouds just split open, and blast, I'd never seen such rain - or so it seemed at the time.

'That was a rum old summer. There was a funny feeling about. Every day you heard of more men out of work, and wages were being cut everywhere. The Corn Production Act, which had guaranteed prices for the farmers, was ended, and so the prices they got were cut as well.

'I remember before that went, I was talking to an old Liberal farmer in Butchers Lane. I think he'd been a schoolmaster before he turned to farming. Anyway, he asked me what I thought of the Corn Production Act, and I told him I wasn't really interested in it. I hadn't got anything to sell. It hadn't made much difference to me. But he was pleased with it. He said, "When I go back and look at my crops I can judge more or less what they'll come to. Then I know exactly how much money I shall have each year. I'm very satisfied with it,"he said, "but if we get a free hand your wages will come down to twenty-five bob."

'But a lot of farmers didn't like the Act. They were silly really, because they were getting a guaranteed price for their corn. But when the Act ended, my word, the merchants gloried in it, because they could make their own price with the farmer, and that year of the drought, when the corn had hardly filled out, the prices came down for the farmers just like the men's wages. Around here the wages dropped from fifty bob (£2.50) to twenty-five bob (£1.25). That were a proper slump. The farmers hadn't got the money, nor had we, and there were more men than jobs to go round. It wasn't until 1930 that our wages got back to thirty bob (£1.50) again.' (These wages were slightly lower than in some other parts of Suffolk.)

'They stayed like that, more or less, until the second world war, and then we got £2 a week. We had to pay a little bit of income tax even on that, but it was refunded after the war. After that our pay went up slowly until by November 1958 we were getting £7 a week, and things were really just good for us. Everybody was satisfied. Unfortunately, I only took it for one week, because the weather set in bad, and I had to pack up work at Christmas, and that was that. But everyone seemed to be in work, and we were satisfied. Oh dear, what a difference there is now - everyone after all they can get. Never satisfied with anything.

'But when the Corn Production Act came to an end in 1921, the farmers soon began to feel it. I don't suppose they could have paid us more if they'd wanted to. Of course, they didn't like the workers' union. They'd got their own union, but they didn't see why we should have one too. And when they had to give us a half-day off on Saturdays, why blast, they didn't like that either.

'Mr Lilley used to laugh at the union. He'd say, "You come to me when you want money, boy." No, he didn't like it. But that did help to improve conditions, there's no doubt about it. Not everyone joined. There was no compulsion. And that was no good a-saying you'd come out on strike, because there was always someone ready to jump into your shoes. Well, I joined for a while, and then I found out that those who weren't in the union were getting just the same money as those who were. So I come out of it. I didn't see much use for it. Farmers round here still didn't pay you if it was wet, even though they should have done. They just did as they pleased.

'Blimey, that's different today, isn't it? If a chap puts in a screw and that's not his job, they all come out on strike. That make me mad, that do. However they can be so simple, I don't know. Just a score of men can chuck a thousand people out of work. That's silly. They don't act like working men today. They act like overgrown schoolboys. Some of them don't deserve jobs, and that's a fact.'

So although in the wheat and barley lands of West Suffolk farmers and farmworkers alike felt the effects of the slump in the nation's economy and the neighbourhood had its quota of workless men, the great convulsion of unemployed that brought demonstrations in other parts of the country scarcely sent ripples into the agricultural villages in this part of Suffolk, and there was never a chance of serious conflict between the unions and the farmers. There was always work for George to do.

In the summer, when there was no threshing to be done, the traction engines were used for steam sawing. Some of Harry Rice's men were kept busy cleaning and overhauling the machines, and others were used for sawing. George was one of them.

'He wouldn't insure all of us, because he said that would be too stiff. He only insured me, and so I was the one that had to use the saw. I liked the job really. We had all the trees that we'd cut out of the hedgerows. Then we'd cut palings, or a gatepost, or a barn door out of them.'

The log or tree to be cut would be drawn up a frame and wound on to the bench with a long chain by hand. The circular saw was driven by a belt from the steam engine to the pulley on the bench. There was no guard to give protection from the screaming revolutions of the saw.

'Sometimes it was just firewood that had to be cut up. There was a man at Layham who had barbed wire along the banks of his fields, and we'd have the job of cutting out stakes for that. Of course they had to have three-sided points so they could be driven into the ground. That was as easy as you like, but my mate, Benny King, he couldn't get the knack of it at all. "Well," I say, "that's easy, Ben. You just stand there and take one bit off, and then you turn it and take another bit off, and then you turn yourself, take off again, and you've got your three bits off. And there's your stake, boy." You could do it as quick as lightning, but you had to be careful of your hands - to keep them out of the way of the saw. It did just clip mine once, but not enough to take my fingers off.

'We used to go to all the villages around here. Sometimes Mr Kemball, here in Boxford, would have a tree that we had to split up for him. He was a carpenter and made the village coffins. He always had oak and elm, but on a farm you had just what came - maple, wild cherry, chestnut. I liked chestnut - that's a lovely wood. To look at it you would think it was oak. When you cut it, that was lovely.

'But the work was a bit rough sometimes. I mean, you'd get what we call a tod tree. [1] That would be awkward, because there were always new shoots of growth coming out of the top, and you had to chop them off before you could get it on the table to split.

'I was quite handy with that saw. Sometimes I've cut out stuff for a handmade harvest wagon, not for the framework, you understand, but for what we call the buck [2] of the wagon. That would usually be elm. Oh, I used to enjoy that work. Wood is such

---

1 Suffolk dialect: The stump of a tree that has been sawn off and left in the ground. Often also applied to the ivy that frequently grows round the tod and provides a place for owls. Thus Beaumont and Fletcher in *Bonduca*:

There valiant and approved men of Britain
Like boding owls, creep into tods of ivy
And hoot their fears to one another nightly.'

2 Suffolk dialect: The body of a wagon. This was usually of elm, with the framework of oak and the shafts made of ash. Sometimes white poplar was used instead of oak for the frame.

a lovely thing to handle. And the job was a sight cleaner than being the sacker at threshing time.'

Sometimes George would cycle from farm to farm, and on other occasions he would drive the Garrett traction engine himself. It was this which ultimately led to his decision to leave Harry Rice. He didn't much like the responsibility of driving the engine.

'No, I didn't relish it really. You'd got to keep steam up; you'd got to keep things regular. That was all right when it was going well, but when the tubes began to leak your fire dulled down and you had a job to keep the steam up. When you opened the door to coal up, you could see the tubes dripping. Well, if you were at work that would keep up pretty well, but once you stopped, p'raps for dinner, that would start leaking again. Then you had a job to get the steam up. That was the reason I left. I got fed up with it. It was too much of a worry. He wouldn't take it off the road to have it seen to. So at the end of the season I left. That was 1926.

'Even before I'd given in my notice I had another job. On my way home one Saturday I thought I'd call in and see Mr Lilley. So I did, and I asked him if he wanted anyone for harvest and if he could give me a job. "Why, are you leaving Harry?" he said. I told him I was, but I didn't know if he'd want to take me back. "Of course I will," he said. So I went back to Mr Lilley, and that was when the half-day off come in. On a Saturday we knocked off at twelve o'clock. He didn't like that much. But I kept with the old chap and got on very well with him after that. I stayed with him until 1931.'

There had meanwhile been some small improvements in the quality of village life, and modest luxuries were becoming available. Towards the end of the 'twenties George bought the family's first radio set, a Marconi. Moreover, he bought it in the village from a shop which had formerly been a saddler's, but was now venturing into the new technology. (Today it is the village newsagent's.)

'It was kept by a young fellow called Peachey, and he sold wireless sets, and would also charge up your batteries. The set I bought ran off an accumulator, and after a bit you had to take it to be recharged. My dear old mother thought that was wonderful. She used to listen to Henry Hall, and she loved the Palm Court programme.'

Already the first garage had established itself in the village. Originally it occupied premises which in more recent times became a bakery, a general store, an antique shop, and is now a private house. But in the 'twenties new premises were built about a hundred yards further up the road.

'The business belonged to the Riddelsdell brothers, and Percy Riddelsdell was the first man in Boxford to have a motor-bike. That would have been before the first world war - nineteen-ten or eleven. But I think they started building the present garage in 1922, and one Sunday morning we had the most terrible gale. Well, that blew the whole framework down, and they had to start again.'

The garage, much redesigned, still trades under the same name on the same site, but there are no Riddelsdells in the business today.

'But you could say that, by the time I went back to work for Mr Lilley, things were really beginning to improve in the village.'

18
Back to Horses

George's return to his old master also meant working with horses again. Tractors were still rare in the arable acres above the Box valley, and it was almost another five years before Mr Lilley bought one. So although George was engaged to do day work he quickly found himself as the odd man with a pair of horses.

He was also expected to take his share in caring for them, but he was never admitted to the secrecy of the horseman's craft. There is a large folklore connected with the care and control of horses, involving the use of secret recipes and even, it is said, magical practices. George was aware of this heritage and of a strange power that certain men were able to exercise over the animals, but his own attitude was both practical and sceptical. He believed in being gentle and kind with a horse, and he then found that they invariably responded to him, and would do what he wanted.

'A lot of it was how they were broken in. All men weren't alike. Some were very rough with horses, and if they were too rough when they broke them in, the horse was always jumpy. You have got to be kind with them when you break them in.

'I've never actually done it on my own, but I've helped the head horseman when he was breaking in colts. I didn't like the job myself. You've got to be very quiet with them. A lot depends on the breed. Some are highly strung, and then you'll get another that's just the opposite, and a bit lazy. We used to lunge them on a rope to start with, and then after a bit we'd put a pad over their backs. That was so they would slowly get used to the idea of having something there. It could be a slow business. Then, when we put them to work on the plough, we'd always put them with an old stager, a quiet one. Some colts would really go right off straight away. They'd take to the work. Others would jump about a bit. Then you had to give them a little bit of kind treatment.

'Some of the old boys, I know, had their secrets, but they'd never tell anyone else. They never told me. They'd have some stuff made up by the chemist, and they just rubbed it on themselves, and the horse would know. He'd follow. That was called drawing a horse.[1]

Conversely causing a horse to stop suddenly and refuse to move was known as jading the horse, and was done by using substances the smell of which the horse found repellent.

'No, I was never taught any of these tricks, but I seemed to be able to manage the horses all right without them. And they kept pretty healthy without any special kind of treatment. I've heard that some people would mix bark from the trees with the horses' food, but we never did that. But the stockman would sometimes break up his linseed cake or cotton cake, that we had to give to the cattle to fatten them up, and we'd put that in the horse food. You see, there was always a certain amount of dust from the linseed. We'd mix that up with the horses' food, and that did bring a shine on their coats. I've done that myself many a time.

'We had a machine to break up the cake. It was a kind of roller with spikes on, and you could set it as close as you like, if you wanted to break up the cakes small. They were a good two feet long and about eighteen inches wide. You put the cake in, turned the handle, and that pressed it down and cracked it.

'You had to look after your own horses, so I had to groom my two in the mornings. In the summer time the poor things would sweat a lot, and that would corrode on their shoulders where the collar rested. Well, you had to get that off otherwise that would make their shoulders tender. I never used any oils or anything special on their coats, not that I remember. But if the shoulders or the withers got a bit tender I would bathe them with salt water. That did wonders for them. So I reckon if a man looked after his horses and kept them clean he never had any trouble. In the summer, of course, they were left out to graze. But in the winter you had to bring them into the stables and straw them up.

'Horses are like men - all individuals, none is the same shape. So when you harnessed up in the morning, each one had his own collar on his own peg. You always put the collar on first, and then the bridle. We called the saddle the pad.'

1   The substance was probably a mixture of aromatic oils - origanum, rosemary, cinnamon and fennel. George Eward Evans in *The Pattern Under the Plough* (1966) records this recipe from an old horseman's notebook, with the instruction: 'Set this mixture by the wind.' A horse with a keen sense of smell was invariably attracted by such an aromatic mixture.

There are other words that George uses for parts of horse gear which may have been peculiar to his area of Suffolk. The breeching, which is part of the horse's harness attached to the saddle and hooked to the shafts, George says was always called 'brichens', and the chains hooked on to the shafts for pulling were called the 'filbert' chains. The words are not given by Moor, Forby or Claxton, but George insists they were in regular use locally.

'There was a saddler and harness-maker in the village in those days.' (The premises are now a newsagent's and confectioner's shop in the broad centre street of the village.) 'Turner was his name. He was a big fat old boy. He had a chap called George Gooch to help him. The old boy was a pretty good saddler too. Do anything for you, he would.

'They were all horse-drawn carts and wagons round here. But there were some people who had hunters to ride around on. So he had a lot of work to do. It must have been in the 'twenties that he finally gave up.

'The hunting folk used to meet here three or four times a year and always on Boxing Day. You'd get officers out from the Colchester garrison with the hunt, and anyone with a horse would follow. I biked round sometimes if I wasn't at work. I liked that. But I don't reckon they caught many foxes. That's hard going over arable land. The foxes weren't really a menace here either. There were plenty of rabbits about for them.'

There was work for four blacksmiths in the neighbourhood, one in Boxford and one each in the neighbouring parishes of Groton, Edwardstone and Polstead. The forge in Boxford was probably the largest, with room for three or four horses. It stood immediately opposite the fifteenth-century flint church in the middle of the village. George, however, invariably took his horses more than another mile up the road to Groton. There were family reasons for doing so. Mr Lilley was married to the sister of tbe blacksmith, Harry Lingley.

'You'd got to be there by six in the morning if you wanted to be the first one to be done. So on those mornings I'd be up at half-past five to give me time to ride there.

'The blacksmiths also had to repair all the farm implements, but when the newer machinery came in that was the end of the blacksmiths. The last one at Boxford forge was a Mr Stone. He was also the church clerk and used to dig the graves as well.'

The building is now a private house with an eighteenth-century frontage hiding the earlier timber-framed construction. The forge itself is still there and is now a feature of the living room. It is used as a raised open fire to burn logs.

Although it had not been George's intention to return to horse work - and he is certain he would not have wanted to be head horseman even if the job were offered to him - he nonetheless enjoyed the relationship between horse and man. Men and horses had worked the land together for centuries, and perhaps it was an awareness of this essential closeness that he found satisfying. In any event he admitted that it was a very fundamental and rewarding relationship. He enjoyed it best when he was walking behind the plough.

But this ancient relationship had inevitably to come to an end. During the war tractors first made their appearance in the local fields, and one man with a tractor and plough went from farm to farm and had a contract with individual farmers to plough their land. Yet once the war was over farmers were slow to introduce the new machinery. Mr Lilley bought his first tractor from a Colchester firm in 1928. It was a Fordson, and with it was a Ransome two-furrow plough. It is scarcely accurate to say that George was taught to drive it, but drive it he did, within a few minutes.

'It came with a leaflet telling you how to carry on. The chap who delivered it said to me, "Have you ever used a horse plough?" I told him, "Why, of course I have." He looked at me and said, "Oh well, then there's no need for me to tell you how to go on. That'll all come to you." Well, we had a couple of bouts together - that's twice up and twice down - and that's all. Then he said, "Now you read this leaflet and that'll tell you what to do." And that's what I did, and I got on very well with it. The only trouble was that it was always a job to start. They didn't have self-starters in those days. You had to crank it, and that blinking thing seemed to be temperamental. Sometimes that would take the best part of an hour to get going. But once it was going that was all right. It had first, second and third forward gears and one reverse. But that wasn't as good as the horses. I know there's a lot of walking to do with horses, and the poor things get tormented with flies in the summer, whereas flies didn't hurt the tractor, but I can't say I loved driving a tractor. That was an easy job, but the smell and the fumes used to put me right against it.'

Although George described the act of ploughing as an easy job, he maintained that it was easier to achieve a straight furrow with a horse than with a tractor.

'With a horse you'd got your hands on the plough itself, and you could put your plough on the back a wee bit and take a smaller furrow, or if you wanted to take a bigger furrow you just pulled it on to the breast. But with the tractor, you just had a plough a-following on behind. You could drive your tractor straight, but that wasn't to say your plough would always follow straight. Of course you had your levers and a little wheel that lifted or dropped the plough-share according to the depth you wanted. Then you'd got another lever if you wanted to take a smaller furrow. You could lever it over and what we called hake[1] the plough off.

'With a two-furrow plough you could do about three acres a day. Mind you that depended upon the length of your land. If that was short land, it took you longer, because you had more turns to make, but if you'd got long land you didn't need to make so many bouts. Of course with a single-furrow plough you wouldn't do more than an acre a day.

'The tractor was the beginning of all sorts of changes. When I started driving the thing my boss said we should have to have bigger stetches. Up to then our stetch had been eleven feet two inches, but now we had an eight-yard stetch. And he wouldn't allow me to shut up, not with the tractor plough, unless he was really pushed and a bit behind with his work. Then he might tell me to shut it up and get it ready. Otherwise I had to leave it in three-furrow pieces for the horseman to come behind and shut up.

'Then as time went on they got different sorts of ploughs, and the field was just ploughed one way and you didn't have stetches at all. But years ago they were so particular about having stetches with the water furrows to take off the top water. Today they don't want any. A field is ploughed all over the same, and then it's harrowed to a fine tilth all over the field without any furrows anywhere. Still, many of the fields around here are well-drained, I'll say that for them.'

During much of George's farming life there were two strains of barley that were mostly grown in his area - Chevallier and Spratt Archer.

---

1 Suffolk dialect. George is using, as a verb, a word normally used as a noun. The hake was sometimes called the bridle or muzzle.

'The Spratt Archer was a flat barley, and I don't think it produced quite as well as the Chevallier. That was a very good malting barley, that was.

'The wheat we grew around here was Little Joss, Red Standard, Squareheaded Master and the Old Kent Red. Then in the 'twenties a new one come out. It was called Yeoman. It had a much shorter straw, and that produced very well that did.

'It was all wheat, barley, oats, beans and peas in these parts. And perhaps we'd sow a few acres down with clover seed in the spring, and then after the harvest that would ley[1] until the next year. Then we'd use the clover for feed or seed, and the ground would be ploughed up and come in for wheat. They always said you got a better quality wheat behind clover and beans. The wheat used to run well and that would weigh better. But after peas - well, that didn't run quite so well.'

Horse-drawn seed drills were introduced in the eighteenth century, but were not very widely used until about the middle of the nineteenth century, and there were even a few places in Suffolk where, up to the beginning of the first world war, seed was still broadcast by hand.

'I've even done that myself, after a field has been drilled, especially on a clover ley. After the headlands had been ploughed, if there'd been a bit too much rain - well, they wouldn't turn about on what had already been drilled. So you just had to take your corn down in a sack and broadcast on the headlands. Then you could have a gang of harrows over it, and that would bury it.

'Beans we would sometimes sow as we ploughed, with a small drill fixed to the plough. Not every furrow, mind. You'd plough about four inches deep and drill one furrow, then miss one, because you don't have to drill beans so thick as other corn.

'Now with wheat the distance between each row would be about six inches. We had a six-foot drill - a Smythe drill drawn by two horses - so that would do twelve rows, but if you were on an eleven-foot two-inch stetch, as I mostly was, then you'd have to block off one counter[2] coming back, because that would be too far over. So you got twenty-three ringes[3] on one stetch.'

---

1 Another example of George's characteristic habit of sometimes using a noun as a verb.

2 Coulter. Neither Moor, Forby nor Claxton give 'counter' as a dialect alternative, but George insists that coulters were always known as counters in his part of Suffolk.

3 Suffolk dialect: rows.

With the advent of the tractor George felt the loss of much of the satisfaction that he had previously derived from ploughing with a couple of horses. Nevertheless he went on tractor ploughing for two or three more years before eventually he left the man who, off and on, had been his master since his school days. There were other reasons than personal dissatisfaction which led to George's departure.

His father had died, aged 71, in January 1929.

'It was a Wednesday when he died. Cancer killed the poor old boy. I remember when I saw him the day before, he said to me, "I've had a lovely dream, George. I dreamt I saw Morris. He had a hole in his forehead, but that didn't spoil the dream. It was lovely to see him again."

'The next day he died. Afterwards, I went to see Fred Elmer, who had been with my brother when he was killed. He told me that, among his injuries, Morris had been shot in the forehead.'

After her husband's death the health of George's mother began to deteriorate. It was this which decided George that he should leave his old master.

'So I left him in 1931. Well, I thought to myself that it was a long way to come home from Bower House Tye, and I used to feel vexed every morning when I went out and left my mother. She'd had a hard life, and I thought I ought to be nearer home.'

19
The New Crop

For the next two or three years George did casual work wherever he could get it. In his neighbourhood this wasn't difficult even in the 'thirties. Daymen invariably found employment as the result of local farmers talking to each other about their labour needs. It was in this way that he came to work on Mr Daking's farm, at the north edge of the village, for the 1931 harvest. He stayed on to lift the sugar beet.

Although today about a quarter of the country's sugar comes from beet grown in East Anglia, the local farmers had been slow in growing the root. It was rare to find anyone in the area growing sugar beet before the first world war, and it spread only slowly afterwards.

'Mr Lilley never did grow any. He didn't think much of it. He always said it was too much bother and there was a lot of waste.

Some people who kept cattle would feed the beet leaves to them, or to sheep. I think originally some Dutchmen came over and showed us how to grow the beet. But that was slow to catch on.

'Sugar beet was drilled in the middle of April. They'd say the 15th of April was plenty soon enough. The Smythe drill was a very handy old drill for sugar beet, because you could have four counters (coulters) twenty-one inches apart - one near the wheel, one next to the wheel, and then the other two were spaced so they were twenty-one inches apart. I think some farmers tried to drill them a wee bit closer. Later on we took the shafts off the Smythe drill and made a steerage for the tractor. You only wanted a light tractor, and then you could go up and down the field lovely with that.

'Today, if the weather's right, they're drilling beet in February. 'Tis true, when you drill early you get more runaways - more run to seed - but they don't seem to mind.

'Harvesting beet was a hard business. We had a beet

plough. It was similar to the ordinary horse-furrow plough but that had a different spit[1] on it so that it would go under the roots and lift them. Then we had to pull them, knock the earth off, put them in rows, and chop off the leaves by hand. We did this with a blade about a foot long, called the beet topper, and you had to cut off just the top of the beet as well as the leaves. That was a cold old job and back-aching too, I can tell you. Around the headlands we had to lift them with a four-tined fork, and if the ground was wet and the plough was slipping, you often had to ease out some of the others with a fork too. Nowadays you've got lifters that cut them off and put them right away on to the wagons. But we had to make heaps of them and cart them off to a dump. Then they'd be loaded on to lorries to take them to the factories at Bury St Edmunds[2] and Ipswich.

'Pulling mangolds was another miserable old job at this time of year. And that had to be done by hand. On a cold damp day your hands would get proper frawn[3], but after a time they'd warm up and you wouldn't notice it any more. Mind, if you stood still for ten minutes or quarter of an hour, your hands would go cold again.

'Mr Daking didn't like you to use a knife to cut the blades[4] off - that's the leaves, you know. We used to call them blades. No, he was afraid cutting them off might damage the crown, and if you cut the crown that would sometimes rot the mangolds. So we had to wring them off. That might have taken a wee bit longer, but I doubt it, because you pulled the mangold out with your right hand, just collared it with your left, and then give it a wring with your right. But if you were chopping the leaves off, well you'd have to change hands. That sounds a slow old job, but you'd be surprised how much one man could do, especially when he was paid so much an acre.

'Once you'd pulled and topped the mangolds they had to be carted and earthed up in clamps. We had to thatch them first with straw, and then earth them up to keep the frost out, because they were used later to feed the cattle. On the top we'd put in a drain

---

1 George is using the word as a synonym of share. In Suffolk a spit is a spade's depth.

2 The factory at Bury St Edmunds holds the European record for the highest tonnage of beet processed in a single season.

3 Suffolk dialect: frozen.

4 Not given by Moor, Forby or Claxton, but it is the word used locally.

pipe, or an old land drain, or you'd get some straw and twist it to make a funnel. That was to let the heat out. Well, it kept me busy until Christmas time. The mangolds and beet were usually in by then, although if the weather was bad it could sometimes be February before all the sugar beet was lifted.'

After Christmas George found work readily enough in Langham - a village in Essex just over the River Stour border. This was the heart of Constable country - indeed, from a spot near the church in this village Constable had one of his favourite views of the Dedham Vale - but it was about seven miles from home, further away than ever before. Nevertheless, the construction of a waterworks to supply the whole neighbourhood, provided work for a large force of men. George's brother Charlie was already working there. For George it was a heavy pick-and-shovel job, digging trenches and levelling them off ready for the pipes to be laid. It kept him employed until February 1933, by which time the waterworks was almost completed.

Throughout the spring and summer George was able to work very much closer to home. On the edge of the village, about half-way to George's birthplace, Mr Elmer Faulkner had nurseries where he grew flowers for seed. (His son still has nurseries on the same site.) George hoed the beds, tended the blooms, and picked the flower seeds until Michaelmas, when he left to do occasional field work for various farmers. Once again he was helping to lift sugar beet, and threshing, on nearby farms.

Meanwhile, his mother's health was worsening. She was weak, and feeling frail and tired. George was more than ever aware of the hard life she had led, and he did all that he could in their small cottage to help with the housework. In the spring of 1934 he returned again to regular farm work. This time it was to a farm of historic interest a little south of the village - Peyton Hall Farm.

The hall itself is a sixteenth-century timber-framed and plastered building standing about a mile and a half south of the village amid the farmland of the Box valley. There are, however, signs of a dwelling on the site much earlier than that, and the family of Peyton derived their name from the manor of Peyton in the parish of Boxford. In the reign of Henry I, it belonged to Reginald de Peyton,[1] and there were Peytons at the hall until 1860, when Sir Henry Peyton sold the whole estate. When George went to work there the farm was managed by John Pawsey on behalf of his father.

It was a farm of over 300 acres, and George was engaged as a dayman. He was one of ten men employed and drew thirty shillings (£1.50) a week for his work. It was a mixed farm of cereal crops and sheep and cattle kept for fattening, but there were no cows. Swedes and mangolds were grown for feed. His working day was from six-thirty in the morning until five o'clock in the evening, and he was expected to be able to tackle any job that came along.

'I did ploughing there with a tractor and a two-furrow plough, although sometimes I had a pair of horses. I liked that better. I think the time may come when we have to use more horses again. I hope that do.

'The fields were bigger than I'd been used to. There was one of a hundred acres, but that was more or less split into three. That was used for growing corn and roots, and that took quite a bit of ploughing, I can tell you, even with two of us on it. The land was a bit hilly, but that was pleasant to work on. Mr Pawsey also kept bullocks, just for fattening up.'

Peyton Hall was evidently 'a rare farm for drains'. In this part of Suffolk, where the land is founded on boulder clay, drainage has always been of great importance - first, bush draining, where a trench was dug a spit deep, and then a narrower spit was taken from the bottom of the trench, and into this was laid brushwood, ideally blackthorn and hawthorn. Tile drains, however, began to be used early in the nineteenth century, although the trench itself was frequently dug in the same way in spite of a number of machines which were invented from time to time. Drains already laid at Peyton Hall George found to be 'at quite a good depth'.

'There was one field with three or four drains that I had to open up because they had become blocked. You could soon tell where the blockage was, because you'd begin to see that spout up or dribble from the soil. Then you could open it up and put in your

---

1 Reginald was possibly a younger son of Walter of Caen, whose father was William Malet. John Kirby in *The Suffolk Traveller* (1732-34) says that Peyton Hall was 'granted by William the Conqueror to Robert Malet, a Norman baron and progenitor of the ancient family of Peyton'. He was the son of William.

rods and free the blockage. Normally, you'd find the drain running in a hollow part of the field, and if the field was sloping, the drain would usually run diagonally across it.

'Of course laying a new drain was hard work. That had to be dug out with draining spades before you put in your pipes.

'But years ago, after a field was drilled with winter corn, we went along with a horse plough and made what we called a water furrow. That'd catch a lot of the top water and take it into the ditches. And there was always a water furrow at the end of each stetch, so the water would come down into the furrow and get away. Today draining is all done by machinery. Why, you hardly need anyone to work on a farm these days. In my time you used to reckon on at least three men to a hundred acres - a lot more at harvest.'

George had been working at Peyton Hall farm for less than a year before his mother, whose health in the preceding months had continued to deteriorate, died at the age of 76 at the end of December 1934. She, more than any other person, had influenced his thought and conduct throughout his life.

'She was buried on the fourth of January 1935. It was a Friday and a very cold day. She was buried in the old churchyard at a little spot above my father. It hadn't been possible to get a double grave because the ground was waterlogged. A few years earlier the Reverend William Andrew[1] said to me, "If you want a little spot just above your Dad, George, why don't you buy it?" So I did. I bought it for £2, and had that saved for my mother. There were a lot of us at the funeral - all my brothers and my sister, and most of the parishioners were there. Everyone turned out to a funeral in those days. They don't trouble much today.'

George went on working at Peyton Hall farm until September 1938. In those late 'thirties, even in the comparative peace of the Suffolk countryside, there was an awareness of threatening war. 'I felt it was going to happen. You could tell somehow.' It was in this uneasy atmosphere of possibly impending shortages that workers were encouraged to keep a pig.

'In some parts of the county there were pig groups, and the members supplied each other with pork. But that didn't happen here. We each kept our own. I had one or two. But I never had one killed for my own use. There wasn't much room to store it. I

---

1 The Revd William Shaw Andrew was Rector of Boxford from 1919 to 1932, when he was succeeded by the Revd Thomas Rice.

used to sell mine to the butcher. But there wasn't a lot to be made out of that. A pig, when you'd fattened it up, made about ten bob (50p) a score (20 pounds' weight). So, if you'd got an eight-score pig, you got about four quid for it. I know the last two pigs I had, I had to give £3 each for them - that was as store pigs just off the sow. Well, I fattened them up and, at that time of day, pigs were making £2 a score, so I thought to myself I should be well away. But I hung on to them a bit too long, I reckon. I got a wheeze that they were dropping. So, at the weekend, I saw the butcher and asked him if he would buy them. By the Monday they'd dropped from £2 a score to fifteen shillings (75p). Well, when it come to it, I actually gained seven-and-sixpence (37 1/2p) out of the two. So I didn't get much, but I didn't lose anything. They were the last pigs I ever had.

'I can't say I ever really had much luck with pigs. Once before, I bought six. My brother-in-law had two of them, and another bloke had a couple, and one of mine died. So I reckon I took a loss on that. That wasn't always easy to fatten them up. You had to watch the food carefully. So I don't know that it was worth the trouble really. Of course some families would sell one pig and get the butcher to slaughter the other for the house, and they might even cure their own bacon, but I hadn't the room for that kind of thing.

'Then, by the time the second war had come, I'd moved on again, this time to my last farm. I was there for twenty years.'

20
His Last Job

George's last employer was Mr Thomas Skinner of Calais Street Corner, on the higher land on the edge of the village. Some of his 160 acres (64.75 hectares) stretched into the parish of Polstead, where George had first begun working on the land.

Tom, as he preferred to be known by his workers, was a stocky man and, according to George, a good man and a good farmer.

'He'd get you anything you wanted for the land. He used a lot of artificial manure. Until then it had been mostly farmyard manure that was put on the land. Oh, he used a lot of that too. But if you wanted artificials, he'd get them for you without any trouble. After all, that was war-time, and we'd got to grow as much as we could. Ah, I liked Tom very much. We liked each other, and I always got on very well with him.'

There were about seven acres of grassland; otherwise, it was an arable farm, growing barley, wheat and sugar beet. Two or three cows were kept, and 'quite a lot' of pigs and bullocks were kept for fattening.

George was mostly employed tractor ploughing, although the farmer also had about six horses - Suffolk Punches and crossbreds, which he used for carting and ploughing.

The Suffolk Punch is a remarkable breed, in various shades of chestnut, with a large head, a deep neck, a great barrel of a chest and a large body. This gives them great strength and drawing power. All of these horses in existence today derive, in the male line, from one horse foaled in 1768, the horse of Thomas Crisp of Ufford.

'Oh, the Suffolks were lovely horses. Now the Shires, they've got a lot of hair round the legs, but the Suffolks are beautiful, clean-legged, and that makes a lot of difference in the bad weather, I can tell you. And they're very strong. They can pull a big weight, they can. And they're so sweet-tempered. There was one stallion there, you never had to tie him up. You just dropped the leader on to the ground, rubbed his nose and had a word with him. Then he'd never move, not till you told him.

'I don't recall that I got a chance to plough with the Suffolks. Tom's son went off into the Air Force, and I had to take over tractor ploughing, and I did that on and off until 1952.

'Of course I had to do other things as well - like grinding up the corn for the pigs and cattle. The pigs were chiefly fed barley, with a few peas mixed in, and all mixed with water. For the bullocks I ground up beans with a little bit of wheat, or oats perhaps. So there were two lots of feed to grind up, and after that I had to crush the oats for the horses.

'During the second war Mr Skinner had about six men working for him, and then women to help with the harvest. They came for the hay-making, and stayed through the harvest to help with the sugar beet. He grew about fifteen acres of it. You were only allowed to grow so much, according to the size of your farm.

'They weren't Land Army girls, just local women, but we did have three German prisoners-of-war on the farm. They were good chaps, and we had no trouble with them at all. They said they were jolly pleased to get caught. They were real hard workers. One of them had been a railwayman, and another had been a farm worker. He was a real strong feller. I liked working with him. I'd get him to help me load up the potatoes. Well, I'd sit on the tractor, and he'd think nothing of lifting hundredweight sacks, and we'd have them loaded in no time.

'You didn't really notice much difference in the village during the second war. The young fellows had to go, 'tis true, but life went on pretty much the same, and we didn't want for anything.

'We had to grow as much as we could, but farming hadn't changed all that much. I know when I began we harvested with a scythe, and now we were using a reaper and binder, and a tractor to do the ploughing. But we were still using horses, and there was a lot of manual labour at harvest time, just as there'd always been. It wasn't really until after the war that the big changes came.

'I gave up tractor ploughing in 1952. I'd never really liked it that much, not as good as ploughing with horses. It was the smell of fumes that would put me off my feed. So one day when Mr Skinner said he'd got a new man coming, I said, "Well, do you put him on the tractor. I'd rather be an ordinary man." And that's what happened. I didn't lose any money over it.

'That was the year that Tom Skinner died, only sixty-two. He died in the same month as King George VI. But I went on working there for another six years. I'd have like to go on until I was seventy, but I had to give up at Christmas 1958. That was arthritis that struck me in the legs, and that was especially bad at harvest time, in September.

'I was on the combine harvester, sacking the corn, when that struck me. The combines hadn't long come in. I think the first around here was about 1955, and I remember thinking at the time, "That's all going to change now. Farming will never be the same again." But that was a very nice bit of machinery. That did away with the stacking for one thing. You hadn't got to worry about that any more, and that was quite a skilful job. I mean you'd got to be a little particular the way you threw up the sheaves. Well, all that time and labour was saved by the combine.

'Of course the first ones were not all that big or as complicated as they are now. I think the first combine on Skinner's farm was in 1957. I never drove it. That was left to Tom's son, Doug. He took over when his father died.

'Well, sacking the corn, you hadn't got a lot of room to move about, and when the sack was full and you pulled it towards you, you gave it a bit of help with your knees, and somehow I must have given them a bit of a wrench. Well, that did me. They had to bring me home on the tractor ... couldn't pedal my bike.

'I had twelve heat treatments for it at the Walnut Tree Hospital in Sudbury. They were given by a Mr White. When he heard I'd be sixty-six the next January, he said, "Be ruled by me, and pack it up. Get a job or two gardening to pass your time, but if you stop on the land, that won't do you a bit of good."

'That was a pity, because I felt fit enough. But I thought to myself that I should get the pension, and so I might as well pack it all up, and do the odd job or two. That's what I did. Chiefly I went up to Mrs Skinner's and did a few hours in the kitchen garden. And I'd go and give a hand at harvest time, although as the combines got bigger and better, there weren't many odd jobs to be done.

'Looking back over it all, I wonder what it would have been like if I'd been a farmer myself. I would have liked that. I've often wished I could be a farmer. But, I mean, the wage you got didn't help you to save. You were working more or less just for your living. There was nothing to put on one side. 'Tis true if I'd been a head horseman, I'd have got a bob or two a week more than the others, but that would never have given me the chance to save two or three hundred pounds. Blimey, that would be like saving thousands today, wouldn't it?

'I didn't feel bitter towards anyone about this. But if I'm honest, I did resent it a little. Yes, I did. I've often thought when I've been at work in the fields, "Well, I keep on work, work, work, and if I could have just got hold of a hundred or two, probably I could have hired a little farm, and worked my way up. That's what I would have liked. But I had to give that thought up. There weren't no chance. They were hard old times as far as money was concerned. On the other hand, we were happy. At least I was. I thought to myself, "As long as you've got something to eat, boy, and just enough to clothe yourself ... well, that's all right." Not like it is today. Blast, they're all craving for money.'

Apart from the odd jobs to be done after he had retired, there was always his own cottage garden, and this was devoted almost exclusively to growing vegetables and dahlias, and he was an expert at both.

'I don't really know how that was I started growing dahlias. I just took a fancy to them. Me and my brother grew a few, and we found people liked them. So we grew some more. Then, after my brother died, I went in for it properly. Sometimes a bus load of people would come down from London, and I'd sell dahlias to them from my back gate.

'Just before the second war, we started having flower shows in Boxford. I used to enter my dahlias and my vegetables. One year I put in twenty-one entries and I got nineteen prizes.

'The flower and vegetable shows began in the park that adjoined the rectory, and they held sports at the same time. Now, of course, the by-pass do run through that. Later the shows were held in the village hall, but they stopped during the war, and although they started up again, they've ceased altogether in recent years. But there weren't many times when I didn't come away with a handy number of prizes.'

For a number of years the two pubs in the centre of the village - the Fleece and the White Hart - had large displays of George's dahlias in their saloon bars.

One of the last occasions when his dahlias had a public

display was for the wedding of a great nephew on Saturday October 23rd 1976. The bride's mother had asked him for enough dahlias to decorate the village hall.

'Well, I told her that was a bit risky expecting dahlias as late as that in this part of the world. I mean we often have frosts long before the end of October. And one frost, and they all go black.'

On the preceding Thursday there was a storm with a lot of wind and rain, but the dahlias survived.

'But afterwards I cocked my eye to the sky, and that had that very clear look. I reckoned there might be an overnight frost. I decided to pick them, but they were so wet that by the time I'd finished I was soaked through. Anyway, I picked five dozen, pink and white. As it happened, we just escaped a frost, but that was a very cold night. The bride's mother arranged the dahlias beautifully in the village hall for the reception. They looked real nice.'

142

21
The Newcomers

The change in agriculture, the decreasing role of the farmer as the main employer of labour in the rural community, has, in its turn, led to a change in the social structure of village life. It is something which George acknowledges but without any suggestion of either bitterness or regret.

'The real change to Boxford, and to the life of the village, came after the second world war. Until then there hadn't really been much change for centuries. I mean most of the people were either born in Boxford or round about. Today that's different. Now, most of them have come from outside. I suppose that's on account of farming having changed the way it have.

'Until the second war the life of most people was connected with the land - the farmers, the farm workers, the local trades and shops. When I was boy, there was nothing but horses around - on the land, carting corn backwards and forwards to the mill. They were used for everything, including carrying from Boxford to Sudbury. There was a nice old boy, a happy old boy, Freddie Bowers, who used to do a bit of carrying with horse and cart. You could go down with him to Sudbury on Thursdays. He was always laughing, always saying something to amuse you. He lived in the middle of the village, and on Saturday, he'd go into Colchester and bring back fried fish, which he'd sell. Of course you had to warm it up when you got it home. But he sold some lovely bloaters too.

'If you didn't go to Sudbury with Freddie Bowers, then you had to go on your bike or walk. At that time, I had to walk.

'We didn't see any motor vehicles getting around until just before the first world war.

'People were different in those days, too. Well, we all knew each other, and we used to help each other a lot. Because of the long working day, most of the gardening had to be done at night and on Sundays, and we'd all exchange things we grew to help each other out. There was a nice friendly feeling. Father grew a rare lot of gooseberries, red currants, white currants and black currants. The birds would get quite a few and, when I was a boy, I had to get up and frighten them before I went off to school.

'You know, this village has never had a squire, not like some others. There's never been the big house and the squire here. Though some people have liked to think they were, 'tis true.

'But there was one man, when I was a boy, that everyone sort of looked up to. That was Sir William Brungate. He lived up School Hill in the old Grammar School.[1] He was the founder of the village hall,[2] and his photograph is still there. He was a really nice gentleman, and he'd got a kind word for everyone. He'd always talk to you. But he wasn't the squire, and he wouldn't have pretended to be.

'There wasn't much to do. Well, we hadn't got the money to do anything. There was a bit of boating on the river Box. You wouldn't think that possible today, but that seemed a bigger river when we had the water mill and the millpool. The mill was burnt down in 1934, and it's been replaced by the doctors' surgery. But I remember in the winter there was skating on the millpool, and Mr Dawson, who was the village watchmaker, had a sleigh, and he used to come down Cox Hill on it. He loved that.

'Then there were the pubs. There were six of them in the village when I was a boy. One of them, the White Hart, even brewed its own beer. Now there are three. In the 'twenties there was one man who would sit in the corner with his accordion playing dance tunes. Some would get up and have a bit of a dance. Then later there'd be a sing-song.

'In the 'thirties there was a fellow at the White Hart who we used to call Tornado Smith. That's because he rode the wall of death at Southend. He brought it to Boxford, about 1935, I think, and had it in the yard there. But I think he started the wall-of-death riding in the 'twenties. He was quite a young lad. And he had a lion, you know. Well, that was a lioness really. He got it when it was a cub. We'd all sit there in the public bar with it, and I've nursed it many a time. But when that got bigger, and I saw it going round on the motor bike. I don't think I'd have wanted to nurse

---

1 A 16th and 17th-century building, now a private house, where Boxford Grammar School was founded under a charter granted by Queen Elizabeth I in 1596.

2 Sir William Brungate KCMG, first chairman and honorary treasurer of Boxford Village Hall. A public meeting on 9th March 1925 took the decision to build the hall, and Sir William headed the building committee. The hall was opened on 15th December 1926. It has recently been enlarged and improved.

it then. That would sit up there, between the handlebars, full grown, and I think that really enjoyed it.

'He'd lead it about the village on a chain. I don't think local people thought much of it. He kept it in one of the back buildings. That was a beautiful creature. I don't know how that came to die. There was a rumour that it had to be shot, but I don't know if that were true. At any rate that was buried just in front of the pub, near where the box tree is.

'Yes, even in those times most of the people hereabouts were local, with names like King, Tricker, Rice, Gunn, Gant, Kemball, Ely, Grimwood, Kingsbury, Whymark and Munson.

'Before the second world war there were only one or two council houses on the edge of the village. Now there are five estates of one kind or another, and the village is full of newcomers, young couples with children, and none of them working on the land. But I think it's nice. They've brought life into the village. They take more interest than we older ones do. After all, they've got their life in front of them. We're on the way out. And it's the new ones who do all the work in the village, and we're more or less content to let things carry on, and leave it to them. That's how I look at it anyhow. I think they've been a benefit to the village, and we're blessed with the kind of people we've got.'

22
'A Happy Life'

George lived at No 6 Butchers Lane, Boxford, until the late autumn of 1979. By then he found that arthritis in his knees made it difficult to negotiate the twisting stairs of his cottage. He moved to 'sheltered' accommodation in a maisonette of his own on a nearby local-authority estate.

His last years in the stud-and-plaster cottage that had been his home since the end of the first world war were spent mostly tending his own garden and giving practical gardening help and advice to his immediate neighbours. He tried to ignore his arthritic pain, but it gave him a rolling gait, more like a sailor than a landsman, as he walked the hundred yards or so for his midday pint at the Fleece or the White Hart.

Early in 1983 George's memories of his life in the early years of the present century helped to form the basis of a play with music performed at the Wolsey Theatre, Ipswich. Entitled *All Women and Bits of Boys* with the sub-title, *Suffolk Memories, 1906-1918*, it was based upon the recollections of those years by local people. Indeed, some 85 per cent of the script owed its origins to transcripts of taped interviews with Suffolk residents. The songs and music used were also written at that time.

The last and most moving speech in the play was based upon George's recollection of the only time he cried during the Great War of 1914-1918.[1] The theatre invited him to a performance during May, one of the few times he had been to a theatre in his life. His verdict was: 'That do take you back. That was really very good.'

From time to time George still returns to his former home and proffers much-valued advice on the cultivation of both flowers and vegetables. He has a similar uncomplicated decisiveness about other matters. He has always kept himself informed on

---

1 See page 99

146

current affairs by assiduous reading of the *Daily Mail*, supplemented in recent years by watching television, and he knows what he thinks about most contemporary happenings. His opinions are mostly rooted in common sense rather than political conviction.

'When we were young we didn't take much notice of politics. I always voted how I thought at the time. Polstead was always Conservative, I think. Boxford was more of a mixture - Conservative and Liberal, and in recent years the Liberals have become Labour. But there was never a lot of active politics in Boxford. They used to have meetings, and that kind of thing, and there'd always be someone to crossgrain them, but there weren't any great election scenes here that I know of. Oh, but I remember now, when I was at school before the first world war, there was Sir Cuthbert Quilter standing as a Conservative, and Heaton Armstrong as the Liberal, and we used to shout out, "Vote, vote, vote for Heaton Armstrong. Stick old Quilter in the mud." But when I got older I didn't have any strong political convictions - just my own opinion, and I went by that.

'I think that's enough for everyday things, but when it comes to what you believe in - well, that's different. I don't know what it was stopped me going to chapel. I never did go to church. I suppose it was getting about with others as we grew older. I liked to take a walk with my mates, Saturday nights especially. I believe in being sociable, and if you can do anyone a kindness, do it, and there'll always come a time when you'll get it back. I think you get rewarded in some shape or form for doing someone a bit of good. That's my way of life anyway. I'm not a greedy feller. I never was. That was my mother made me like that. "Even doing a little for someone," she used to say, "will make your life happy." Some people wouldn't do a thing for you. That was never my motto. I'd always do what I could for anyone. Whether I got anything for it or not, that didn't worry me, not a bit. And never did, not even today.

'My poor old mother lived through hard times. I suppose I had more sympathy with her because of that. But my father worked hard to keep us going, that he did. All through my young life we sort of lived, more or less, from hand to mouth. And the fact that you didn't get paid when it was wet meant that you could lose two or three days a week sometimes. Then you never did get a chance to make the money come level.

'I think those early days on the farm were the hardest times, but I've had a pretty happy life. And I don't think I've ever got into any real scrapes. I don't believe in that myself. That's not the way to lead your life. I'm no angel, 'tis true, but I like to get through life happily. To lead a miserable life, I think is awful.

'Sometimes, you know, I wonder about God. It's the old problem - suffering. Sometimes I think there isn't one. I mean, you take Northern Ireland. Why don't He stop things like that? That make you wonder if there is a God at all. But I do think there's a life after this one. Well, I remember when I had this operation on my ear, I sort of half come round and asked the nurse for a drink. "All right," she said, "I'll get you a cup of tea, and then you'll feel better."

'And when she left me, I went off. I was sensible, though I was weak, 'tis true, but I knew I was gone. Well, you've heard of the valley of death. I went up there. It was a dark, very dark valley, and I walked up there, and when I come to the end, there was a beautiful bright light, like a golden sunset with a halo over the top, and I thought to myself, "How lovely," and I never felt so happy in all my life as I did then. That was the happiest ever I was in this life. I can't really describe that happiness. I stood there, and all of a sudden my mother come right up to me, and she gave me a nice smile, and put out her arms to me, and I put my arms out to embrace her. And then I felt a little tug, and the nurse was saying, "You must swallow this," and I was coming to my senses again. "You must swallow this," she said. So evidently that was running out of my mouth, and I thought to myself, "Yes, I must," and I finished it off.

'Within five minutes I felt a different feller, but I just hadn't got the strength to open my eyes. That was about midday, and when I felt a bit better I told the nurse about the experience. "That's a good job you brought the tea," I said, "because another five minutes and I should have been gone." "Oh no," she say, "I weren't going to let you die." She were a nice little nurse, and I never knew her name.

'Before all this happened I used to think that when you were dead that was that. But that experience made me think that we do meet again. You see, I saw my mother so plainly. Whether I should have died or not, I don't know. That could have all been the effects of the anaesthetic, but I don't think so. At any rate, I'm not afraid to die, not after that, because I seem to know what it is like. But I don't want a long illness, or anything like that. I should like to go nice and quick. But I thought, after I'd come round, I laid there and I thought to myself, "That would have been lovely if I'd gone right off then." I've often thought of that since. Yes, I often think that.

'So I don't know about God, but I don't believe we die.'

Epilogue

As this book was being finished George Everett died. He didn't, as he had wished, go 'nice and quick', but after a comparatively short illness. Those few weeks in hospital at Sudbury were spent in a mood that varied between resignation and impatience.

When he was weakening, he was clearly resigned to facing death, and there was no suggestion that he was in the least afraid. Then, in a period when he seemed to rally his strength, he showed a considerable impatience to get home again, and to resume a life in which he had found happiness and contentment.

He died on May 16th 1984, and his funeral service was held on May 23rd in the fifteenth-century church of St Mary, Boxford.

His dahlias still bloom in the garden which he had tended most of his life.

● ● ● ● ● ● ● ● ● ● ● ● ● ●